T.

THE WRIGHT BROTHERS AND THEIR SISTER

by

Lois Mills

CHRISTIAN LIBERTY PRESS

A publication of
Christian Liberty Press
502 West Euclid Avenue
Arlington Heights, IL 60004
www.christianlibertypress.com

Written by Lois Mills
Revised and edited by Michael J. McHugh
Cover Design and layout by Bob Fine
Copyediting by Diane Olson
Clip art images on pages i, 3, 50, 68, and 140 are copyrighted to Dover Publications.

ISBN 978-1-930092-33-4
      1-930092-33-4

Printed in the United States of America

Ad maiorem

Dei gloriam

CHRISTIAN LIBERTY PRESS
502 West Euclid Avenue
Arlington Heights, IL 60004
www.christianlibertypress.com

Author's Note

I wish to acknowledge gratefully the assistance of Mr. Raymond H. Rice, vice president and chief engineer of the North American Aviation Company, in the preparation of this book. Mr. Rice checked the manuscript for technical errors and made valuable suggestions regarding the explanation of the theory of flight.

My thanks are also due to Mr. Charles E. Taylor, maker of the engine for the first powered flight, for permission to use his account of scenes in the Wright Cycle Shop during the experiments preceding the successful flight at Kitty Hawk.

Mrs. I. C. Shafer graciously shared with me memories of her childhood in Dayton, where her family and the Wrights were friends. I appreciate, too, her kindness in arranging for Mr. Taylor to read the manuscript.

Two friends I name with gratitude for their constant interest in this book, Norma Landwehr Bowles, who assisted in research, and Elaine St. Johns, who gave valuable criticism and advice.

Lois Mills

1955

To Carol

"For there is no friend like a sister,
in calm or stormy weather."

Christina Rossetti

"We were [blessed] enough to grow up in an environment where there was always much encouragement to children to pursue intellectual interests; to investigate whatever aroused their curiosity. In a different kind of environment, our curiosity might have been nipped long before it could have borne fruit."

—*Orville Wright.*

"Isn't it astonishing that all these secrets (of flight) have been preserved for so many years just so we could discover them."

—*Orville Wright, 1903*

PREFACE

*T*he *Story of the Wright Brothers and their Sister* is a wonderful example of how Almighty God chooses to use the foolish things of this world to confound the wise. It is nothing short of a miracle that the two sons of a little known Christian minister, experienced only in bicycle repair and largely self-educated, would be responsible for unlocking the secrets of flight to a waiting world.

It should come as no surprise, however, that these simple and quiet young men did not achieve their success alone. They had the constant support of loving parents and a caring sister, and above all they had the help of the Lord.

Young people need to understand that God can and does bless the efforts of humble and industrious people, young and old alike. The Wright brothers were committed to being useful; they dared to live their God-given dreams even in the midst of public ridicule and financial poverty. They discovered the great thrill of overcoming trials and problems through humble, childlike faith and determination.

May the following story inspire all of God's children to dare great exploits for the glory of Jesus Christ and the good of mankind.

Michael J. McHugh

2005

CONTENTS

ONE: THE TOY

Bishop Wright took a deep breath as he stepped down from the train. How good it was to fill his lungs with the clean, crisp evening air after his long ride in the soot-filled coach!

"Drive you home, Reverend? Only ten cents anywhere in town," called the station carriage driver as he flapped the reins over the back of his bony horse.

Milton Wright hesitated. "It is a long way," he thought. "If I walk, the children may be eating supper, and I'll have to wait to give them their presents." But he shook his head and said, "No, thank you, I will walk." He had spent too much money already. He must not pamper himself.

"Will they like what I am bringing?" he wondered. The handkerchiefs—maybe his wife would have liked a drafting board better. She was always drawing plans for the boys. "I know Sterchens will like her doll. It's easy enough to choose a gift for a little girl." Father Wright smiled as he thought of his young daughter.

But what about the present for the boys? He had thought about it so many times as he rode in the slow train. "Will my son Wilbur like it as well as a book? Is Orville too young to play with it?" he asked himself.

He wanted this to be the best gift he had ever brought them. Even though they did not talk about it, he knew they had not wanted to move to Cedar Rapids, Iowa, this summer and leave their friends in Dayton, Ohio. They understood, of course, that a minister's children could not choose where they would live. They had to go wherever the church sent their father. But Bishop Wright knew his sons had missed the boys they played with.

"Maybe they would have liked separate presents better," he thought. But this was an expensive toy. He really could not afford to buy another.

Bishop Wright had not written to tell his family when he would return, for he wanted to surprise them. For this reason, the three Wright children had been playing out-of-doors ever since the boys had come home from school.

The bright leaves were falling from the maple trees in front of their house, and Will and Orv had raked them into piles and made a bonfire. Sterchens laughed as she ran after them, kicking and scuffing the leaves to hear them crackle when she stepped. Indian summer was over now, and the October twilight was short and the wind chilly.

"Time to come in, boys. It's too cold to play out now. Will, Orv, bring Sterchens. Supper's almost ready," Mother Wright called from the door of the warm kitchen.

None of them wanted to go in the house to sit by the stove. It seemed dull after the leaping flames of their beautiful bonfire. But when they smelled the steak and potatoes frying over the hot wood fire in the kitchen, they were so hungry they thought they could not wait another minute.

The children's names were really Wilbur, Orville, and Katharine, but their mother called them by the names they called each other—Will, Orv, and Sterchens. The boys had given Katharine her special family name when she was a baby. They heard someone call her *Schwesterchen,* which is German for "Little Sister." Katharine's brothers could not remember all of the word, but they liked it. So they called their sister "Sterchens."

Will, who was eleven, and the oldest of the three, helped his mother to hurry supper by setting the table. Then he settled in the corner to read a book of Greek legends that he had found in his father's study.

Orv was only seven years old, so he could not read much. He went into the kitchen to watch his mother as she moved about quickly in the yellow light from the oil lamp on the table. He pulled a wooden chair close to the table and climbed upon it, kneeling, so that he could see his mother's face as he told her about all he had done that day.

Mother Wright's cheeks were pink from the heat of the stove. She looked young and pretty with her brown hair drawn back smoothly into a heavy knot, and her deep blue eyes, so like his own, twinkled with amusement as her son talked. "How excited he gets over everything," she thought.

Four-year-old Sterchens sat on the floor of the living room playing with an almost worn-out cloth doll, which her grandmother Koerner had sent her at Christmas.

Suddenly, the front door was opened and closed again. Then there was a thump on the hall floor as if someone had put down a bag or a heavy package.

Sterchens heard it first and jumped up quickly.

"It's Father, it's Father come home!" she called as she ran into the cold, dark hall. Soon she rode back into the living room on Father Wright's shoulder.

Will laid down his book and ran to the kitchen door.

"Mother! Orv!" he shouted. "Come, Father's home!"

His mother hurried in, drying her hands on her blue gingham apron. Orv dashed ahead and flung himself on his father. Father Wright lifted Sterchens from his shoulder and gave each of the others a kiss and a hug.

Quickly he opened his bag and took out some packages wrapped in strong, brown paper. When Mother Wright saw them she said, "Wait until after supper, Milton. It is ready."

But the children begged to open the packages. Seeing how eager they were, Mother Wright started toward the kitchen. She knew they wanted to see the gifts their father had brought them all the way from New York City.

"All right, all right, just a minute," she said, laughing. "I'll pull the food to the back of the stove so our supper won't burn up."

Her husband followed her into the kitchen, a thin package in his hand.

"Here, my dear, I'm more impatient than the children. Please open it right away."

When Mother Wright opened the package and saw the fine linen handkerchiefs in a fancy box, her eyes filled with tears. She knew her husband must have denied himself necessities on the trip so that he could bring back these gifts.

"Don't you like them, Susan? I thought you could carry them to church and to Missionary Society meetings," Father Wright said anxiously.

"Of course, I like them," Mother Wright said, "but you shouldn't, you really shouldn't, Milton. They are just beautiful, so fine and dainty. But all the present I ever want is to have you safe at home again."

With a sigh of relief, Father Wright took his wife's hand and led her back into the living room.

Sterchens was too happy to say a word when she saw the beautiful little doll that was in her package. It was a real store doll in a starched dimity dress. Its cheeks were very pink, and its eyes were blue and shiny.

Politely, Will and Orv looked at the doll and stood waiting for their present.

"Now, boys," Father Wright said, stepping into the hall, "I brought you something together."

The boys looked curiously at each other as they heard their father opening a package. They watched eagerly for him to come back into the living room. As he came in the door again, he threw something into the air. This something flew about the room, bumping against the wall and hitting the low ceiling.

"Oh, a bird!" Sterchens called out in excitement.

"No, Sterchens, it's a bat," said Orv positively.

But Wilbur watched it with a puzzled look on his face until it fluttered slowly to the floor. Then he picked it up and looked from it to his father.

"What is it, sir?" he asked as he held the wings of paper and bamboo lightly in his hand.

"The man who sold it to me called it a 'helicopter,' Son. He said it is a new sort of scientific toy just over from Paris."

"But what makes it go? What makes it fly?" asked Orv, who always had to know the whys and hows.

"See," Father Wright said, taking the helicopter from Wilbur. Both boys bent over for a close look. "First, I twist this rubber band. That makes these two small fans whirl around and push the toy through the air."

"Like the propellers on a boat," Orv said quickly.

"Yes, just like propellers," Will agreed.

"That's right, boys. That's the idea," Father Wright said heartily. He was pleased and a little surprised to see how quickly his sons understood his explanation.

Just then Mother Wright called, "No more play now, boys. Supper is on the table."

Will and Orv were so excited over their present that they could scarcely be quiet while their father said grace. And tonight he said a longer one than usual. After a blessing for the food, he prayed for "our absent dear ones, Reuchlin and Lorin," his two sons who were away at college.

When he finished, the boys, ignoring their food, asked him so many questions about the helicopter, that their mother finally said, "I declare, you haven't even looked at your plates, boys. Sterchens and I are almost ready for our pudding. Now eat your suppers and let your father eat his."

Father Wright smiled at his sons.

"Your mother is right. Besides, I have told you everything the man who sold it to me said. You'll just have to figure it out for yourselves. After all, it's only a toy."

When they were in bed that night, the two boys went on talking about their amazing gift.

"Let's make another one," said Orv.

"We could measure this one and try," replied Will, who was always more cautious.

"Now—tell me the story you read tonight," said Orv eagerly, as he twisted until he made a comfortable hollow in the feather bed.

Tonight's story was the Greek legend of Daedalus, who made wings for himself and his son, Icarus, from feathers fastened in wax. At last, the boys fell asleep, thinking of Daedalus and of their new toy.

In fact, Will and Orv thought of nothing but their new toy during the next few days. They flew it in the house, they flew it out-of-doors, and they fairly tore it to pieces trying to see how it was made. When the light paper was so torn from the bamboo framework that the helicopter could not be made to take to the air again, they set about making another. To their joy, the copy flew as well as the original.

Sterchens neglected her new doll to tag at her brothers' heels. She squealed with delight every time the curious plaything made one of its wild, wobbling flights. "Of all the games I have shared with Will and Orv, this was the best of all," she thought.

It was such fun to play with their new toy that the boys decided to make one twice as large. But this was a failure. No matter how they tried, they could not make it fly. Puzzled, they put the toy aside. There were other things to amuse them now. It was cold enough for winter sports and for pulling Sterchens on the little sled that Mother Wright had made for her.

The toy was put aside, but it was not forgotten; nevertheless, it would be many years before Will and Orv would solve the puzzle.

Two: A Happy Home

During the next few years, Father Wright moved his family to Indiana and finally back to Dayton, Ohio. He was not a minister with a church of his own but was a bishop of the United Brethren Church. He traveled about the country overseeing the work of churches in Ohio, where he lived, and in other states, as well. Sometimes he was away for months.

Born in a one-room log cabin, Bishop Milton Wright had grown up in the tradition of a pioneer.

Like Lincoln, he studied by the fireplace in the light from pitch pine knots. Work on the farm was hard, for his father used oxen and a wooden plow, but young Milton finally earned enough in this way to attend a small church college called Hartsville. His years there only increased his desire to learn, until he was not happy unless he could be surrounded by books.

Volunteering for missionary work after graduation, he was sent to teach in a church school in Oregon. When he found he would not be allowed to take his books with him on the difficult journey across the Isthmus of Panama, he packed them in a great box and sent them to this wild new land in a sailing vessel, which went all the way around Cape Horn.

Shortly before leaving for his frontier post, Milton Wright met Susan Catharine Koerner, three years younger than he, and still a student in Hartsville College.

"I am going to be lonely way out there in Oregon," he said, "please promise that you will write to me."

"But you will have your books," Susan replied with a teasing smile. After all, she was a little weary of hearing her English professor's constant praise of this former student. She liked to read, but not all of the time. It was in the practical courses where she shined, in mathematics and in science.

"Anyway, what could I write about? I hear that life is very exciting in the Oregon Territory with Indians, buffaloes, and bears. Nothing exciting happens here."

"You could write about the college. I'd always be glad to hear about the college." The young man hesitated and cleared his throat. He did not wish to seem bold. "You could write about you. I'd always be very glad to hear about you."

Although the packet ships brought few letters from her, Milton Wright could not forget the rosy cheeks and sparkling eyes under Susan's lace-frilled bonnet. Nor could he forget her merry laugh and quick wit, and the feeling of comradeship that had grown during their brief acquaintance. As he sat in his bare room in the mission school, he realized that even his beloved books were not enough to bring him happiness, so he dared to write some of his thoughts to Susan. Finally, as soon as his term was completed, he returned to Indiana to persuade her to marry him.

The farm on which Susan lived with her parents was large and well-managed. There were in all a dozen neatly painted buildings. One of them was Father Koerner's carriage shop. Here he manufactured carriages and farm wagons of such fine quality that his fame as a skilled mechanic was known in other states, as well as in Indiana.

"Too bad Susan isn't a boy," he often thought when his daughter came to watch him as he worked in his shop. Sometimes he let her help him, and he was amazed at the ease with which she handled his tools. Why, he scarcely had to tell her what to do! She just seemed to know!

ully, he recalled these days as he stood on
side his wife waving good-bye, while the
_. and groom drove away after their simple wedding. Then he thought of the future.

"How can she leave this comfortable home to go away with a penniless young minister? Of course, Milton is as fine a young man as I've ever seen. There is that to remember, and it is an honor to be a minister's wife."

"Don't worry, John," the bride's mother said, slipping her arm through his as they watched the buggy disappear down the dusty road. "We started with very little, and we've always been happy. Susan will know how to make a happy home."

"That is my only wish for her, that she make a happy home," said Father Koerner.

Immediately after her wedding in 1859, Susan did make a happy home. For no matter how often she and Milton moved to a different house, their home was the same. It was the same in their love and consideration for each other and in their partnership of Christian ideals for the children who were born to them.

But a special feeling of belonging in a place, as well as to each other, came to the family when they moved to the house at 7 Hawthorne Street in Dayton. This house through the rest of their lives was "home" to the Wrights.

The house was small, but it was large enough. It was a frame house made from wide clapboards painted white, with green shutters at the windows and wooden shingles on the roof. Just outside the back door, there was a well with a wooden pump.

While they were moving in, their father called Will and Orv and showed them the pump and the large wood-box on the back porch.

"Now, boys, this is your job. I don't ever want your mother to carry in wood or water while I am away."

So Will and Orv took turns bringing wood from the shed, where it was piled. They took turns, too, working the long pump handle up and down and carrying water from the well for their mother to use in the kitchen.

When the dray that brought the Wrights' furniture from the railway station backed up to the porch, the three children wanted to help unpack. They got in the way of the men who were car-

rying in the heavy stoves and beds until they spoke gruffly to Mrs. Wright.

"Lady, can't you keep your children out from underfoot?"

"Yes, children," Mother Wright said nervously, "you *must* stay out of the way."

"But what can we do, Mother? What can we do now?" the three asked together. "Please let us help."

Mother Wright looked about her with dismay. The living room was filled with boxes and barrels. Opening barrels of dishes packed in excelsior was no task for children, but surely there was something they could do.

By this time, Wilbur was reading his mother's careful handwriting on the labels of the boxes.

"These say 'Books.' Why can't we unpack the books?"

"Of course, you can, boys; and Sterchens can help, too. It's quite a job to unwrap each one. Your father always packs them so carefully." Mother Wright gave a sigh of relief. She knew her children would be busy for some time.

Will and Orv puffed and panted as they carried Bishop Wright's heavy books of theology and philosophy upstairs to his study and piled them on the shelves around the walls.

They had noticed that there were low shelves around two walls of the living room, too.

"Now there will be a place for the books we like, where we can get at them whenever we want to read," Orv exclaimed happily. "And for Sterchens's books, too," he continued.

"Yes, let's give Sterchens the bottom shelf so she can reach the books herself," Will agreed.

Her brothers patiently sorted out her picture books and fairy tales and helped her arrange them on her shelf.

Some of the volumes that the boys placed on the shelves downstairs had worn covers, for they had made the two-way journey around the Horn. Others were more recent purchases. All were books which interested them and which the family would read together.

Plutarch's *Lives*, Addison's *Essays*, a set of Sir Walter Scott's novels, Boswell's *Life of Johnson*, Green's *History of England*, and a set of scientific books—these favorites must be within easy reach.

When the boys unpacked the cumbersome set of the *Encyclopaedia Britannica*, Will thought it should be carried upstairs to their father's study.

But Orv insisted that it be kept downstairs. "Then we can look up things—even when we're eating. If there's something we don't know, we can look it up." And so the Encyclopaedia was always at hand to settle the questions that constantly arose in this inquiring household.

When the stovepipes had been fitted to the stoves and the dishes and pots and pans were in place on the cupboard shelves, Mother Wright realized that she was tired. She sat down wearily in the kitchen.

Then she jumped up. "I'm going to make hot biscuits for supper," she announced with a determined air.

"But, Mother, you're so tired," Bishop Wright protested.

"We're all tired. The children have worked, too. Hot biscuits will make it seem we're really living again," she replied in a do-not-argue-with-me tone of voice.

And it was not long before the Wrights were really living in their home. In a few days, the flowered ingrain carpet was cut to fit the living room floor and tacked tightly around the edges. There were new lace curtains for the windows and some new cushions for the worn sofa. Nothing else in the room was new and everything, old and new, was simple. As for hanging wall decorations, Mother Wright had no patience with the painted pie tins and frying pans, which were in vogue at that time. Since she did all of her own housework and sewed for her family, too, she had no time for dusting useless ornaments. She believed that pans belong in the kitchen, where they were used.

Soon, everything was in its place. Magazines and the latest church papers were lying in neat piles on the golden-oak center table. The old, carved clock that had belonged to Mother Wright's Swiss ancestors was ticking on the shelf beside the family Bible.

All was in order. All was ready. Uncluttered by needless trinkets, there was space here for thoughts, big thoughts.

Three: PARTNERS

O n Sterchens's sixth birthday, her brothers decided that she was old enough to be their partner.
Up until now, it seemed to Will and Orv that they
had been partners all of their lives. Of course, they
played with other boys, but they found that they were
happiest when the two of them did things together.
They also felt they were partners with their mother
and father. Mother Wright was never too busy to talk

with them and answer their questions; and when Father Wright was at home, he was always ready to play games with his sons. Now Sterchens was to be a member of this special group; they were all partners in the truest sense because their minds and hearts were bound together. From this time on, their sister was never left out of her brothers' plans.

There was no begging for money in the Wright household. It was a fixed rule that the children should earn the money for their hobbies themselves. This they did by engaging in a succession of projects—on Saturdays and during vacations. The first project in which Sterchens joined was the scrap-iron business.

How proud she was her first morning, as a partner! Her short legs had to run to keep up with the boys' strides, as they pulled Orv's wagon through the alleys and across vacant lots. But her sharp eyes spied almost as many old horseshoes and pieces of rusty iron as her brothers found. When the wagon was full, the three took their load to the junkyard. Dumping the old iron on his scales with a great clatter, the junkman reached in his pocket and gave a few pennies to each of the boys. Sterchens's eager interest in the transaction changed to disappointment. She struggled to keep back the tears. She must not cry. But Will and Orv had said she was a partner. The boys counted their pennies.

"Great," said Orv. "Here, Will, take mine. You're the banker. Nine cents apiece. That's eighteen cents toward our woodcarving set."

Hearing a little sniffle, the older boy looked down at Sterchens.

"No, Orv," he said gravely. "You haven't counted right. That's twelve cents toward our set," and, winking at his brother, Will dropped a third of the pennies in the pocket of Sterchens's red pinafore.

When her brothers took the wagon to the woods at the edge of town to gather nuts after the first frost, the little girl went along. Although she could only pick up the ones that had fallen on the ground, she hopped about happily until she had filled her apron. Then she added her small gathering to the nuts Will and Orv had picked. On reaching home, the boys carefully separated the nuts into three equal piles.

Sterchens could not share in all of the boys' efforts to raise money for their hobbies, but they always made her feel that she had a part in them. When they made kites to sell, she went along to the hill above the river where they tried them out.

She stood with her heart beating fast in excitement as she saw the creations of her brothers' clever hands rise like birds in the wind.

Stilts that they made were in great demand by other boys who saw them because they could be used upside down to gain greater height. So that Sterchens should not feel left out, they made a special, small pair of stilts for her.

When school was out in the summer, the three shared many pleasures. But most of all it was their picnics in the woods that Sterchens liked. Will and

Orv loved to cook out-of-doors. They had a secret picnic spot where they had set up a crude grill made from some old pieces of iron. Mother Wright let them take along bacon to broil over their fire and potatoes to bake in the coals. Sterchens smacked her lips, just thinking about it.

But Will and Orv were not satisfied. As they were starting for the woods one day, Will complained, "It takes too long to get the fire going."

"And it smokes too much," Orv added.

Then, as often happened in the years to come, they thought of the solution together.

"I know what we need," Will said.

And before he could finish, Orv shouted, "A chimney! We could make one from tin cans. Fit them together like stovepipe joints."

Leaving Sterchens standing on the sidewalk, the boys ran to the trash bin in the backyard to get the cans they needed for their experiment. Nothing her brothers did surprised Sterchens, and everything they did was wonderful.

When they reached the picnic spot, she gathered twigs and small pieces of wood to keep the fire going while the boys put the cans together to make a chimney.

"It works," panted Orv, his face red from the heat of the coals.

"It sure does," Will chuckled, giving his brother a slap on the back. "Inventors, that's what we are."

Sterchens was proud of the invention, too, but the part of the picnic she liked best was listening to the stories Will told as they lay on the grass after their lunch. Sometimes he made up funny stories to make them laugh. Sometimes he told them a story from one of the books he was reading.

Some of the neighbors thought Will was lazy because he read so much. When Mother Wright heard them say this, it made her angry. She knew how much Will did to help her in the house. "He's just quiet, that's all," she defended him fiercely. "You just wait. You'll see. That boy has powder under his heels."

"Orvie is too busy to read," she would add under her breath. And who would know this better than his mother? He was seldom quiet and was full of mischief. He was always trying to make some new thing. Often he did not finish his experiments, but fortunately Mother Wright was a patient woman. She let him clutter up her kitchen until it was sometimes hard for her to cook. But she let him keep on using the kitchen as a laboratory. She did not tell him whether or not his ideas were of use but left him to find it out for himself.

Each child had a share in the housework. Orv and Sterchens received five dollars apiece on New Year's morning for doing the dishes through the year. Their father put the shining gold pieces under their plates, and they felt very rich for several weeks. Will helped his mother with the heavy work of laundry and scrubbing, for she was often ill during these years.

Although Will was four years older than Orv, they were about the same size as they were growing up. They played baseball together, did stunts on the horizontal bars, and ran on the track team at school.

Sometimes, Will would tease his brother until the younger boy was almost ready to fight.

"I like to scrap with Orvie," he used to say, "because I like to scrap with a good scrapper." But Will was quick to defend Orv if anyone else tried to threaten or tease him.

Sterchens was growing, too, but she still loved her dolls. Her brothers put their money together and gave her one on each of her birthdays and at Christmas. The year she was ten, Orv saw a beautiful doll in a shop window. "Wouldn't Sterchens love a doll like that?" he asked himself. "Not a girl in Dayton would have a finer one. Anyway, it would not do any harm to go in and ask the price."

Carefully, the shopkeeper lifted the doll from the window, gently smoothing her pale blue satin dress. He glanced at the price tag and then looked quizzically over his spectacles at the eager boy.

"Well, now, this really is a doll. Opens and shuts her eyes. Dress is made out of real satin."

Orv could not bear the suspense. He interrupted the man's praises. Anybody could see it was a perfect wonder of a doll.

"But how much does it cost?"

"Two dollars, son."

"Two dollars! Whew!" He might have known. Sadly, he shook his head.

"Didn't want to go that high, son?" the shopkeeper asked in a sympathetic tone. "Well, it's a long time to Christmas, anyway."

The sympathetic tone gave him hope, and the shopkeeper's remark gave him an idea. "It is a long time to Christmas," Orv thought, several months in fact. If he saved his allowance until then—quickly he figured. He could just make it.

"Say, would you lay it away for me and let me pay you some on it every week?"

The shopkeeper considered the proposition.

"One of Bishop Wright's boys, aren't you?"

"Yes, sir, I'm Orville," he answered in his most polite manner.

"Want the doll for your sister, I suppose?" the man continued.

"Yes, sir, for Sterchens."

Orv watched his every move as the shopkeeper reached under the counter for a paper box and laid the fragile doll in it.

"All right, son, I'll put her away for you; and when she's paid for, you can take her home."

If there were no customers in the shop when Orv came to make his weekly payments, the man behind the counter would open the box to let him gaze on the doll's china beauty. Each time he saw new charms—the eyelashes, so carefully pasted on, the bright blue eyes that did in fact open and shut, the pearly teeth, the thick curls of real hair. The thought of Sterchens's joy was almost more than he could bear. He felt that Christmas came and went each time he visited the shop.

Late in the afternoon before Christmas Eve, Orv went to the shop with his last payment. The package was ready for him, and the shopkeeper heartily wished him a "Merry Christmas."

"Merry Christmas," the boy replied as he dashed through the door and pushed his way through the crowd of last-minute shoppers. He clasped the package carefully in his arms as he began the icy mile and a half walk to the house on Hawthorne Street. He could not believe it! This was the doll—Sterchens's doll. Where could he hide it? How could he ever wait until morning to give it to her?

He could not, or at least he did not. Sterchens was helping Mother Wright make popcorn and cranberry strings for the little Christmas tree when Orv came into the warm living room.

"What do you want for Christmas?" he shouted as he unwound his long woolen muffler.

He had asked this question each day, so Sterchens twinkled at her mother and replied as she had each day, "A doll."

Thrusting the package in her arms, Orv said in triumph, "Well then, open this."

He could not wait another minute.

Four: BIG BUSINESS

Mother and Father Wright kept a steady stream of new ideas flowing through their home. When Fridtjof Nansen was astonishing the world by his daring sled trips to unknown parts of the world, and Lieutenant Robert E. Peary was making his hazardous attempts to reach the North Pole, so real was the interest of the Wright family that it seemed they might almost be living in the polar regions instead of in their cozy house in Dayton. And so it was with discoveries in the world of science, as well. Whatever engaged the attention of one was important to all.

The children were so busy and so happy at home that they seldom went anywhere else to play. Home, with all that went on there, was more interesting than any other place to the five Wrights. And so, they stayed at home in the evening.

After the supper dishes were cleared away, the boys would get out their engraving set or their woodcarving tools. When Father Wright was at home, he read or played a game of dominoes with Sterchens before it was time for her to go to bed. Mother Wright sat with her sewing near the table where the boys were at work, so she could answer their questions or give advice if they asked it. At first, the things that Will and Orv made were of no use at all. But as they became more skilled in handling their tools and learned more about how different woods may be used, they were even able to make a chair for their mother.

One evening, the boys were busy with their woodcarving.

Suddenly, Orv put down his tools. "What we need now is a lathe," he said. "Then we could make things faster and make bigger things, too," he continued.

"Handwork is slow," Will agreed, "but where can we get a lathe? Machines cost money, Orv."

"We could make one," the younger boy insisted stoutly. "There are plenty of big pieces of maple in the barn for the framework."

"But where could we find out how to use them?" his brother asked. "We would have to have a plan before we could even begin."

Orv knew in his heart this was true, but he could not bear to give up the idea. All at once, he remembered that their Grandfather Koerner had a wood-turning lathe in his shop. Perhaps their mother could tell them how to make one like his.

"Mother, tell us about Grandfather Koerner's lathe. We could make one, couldn't we?"

His mother glanced up in surprise. "Make one, Orvie? Perhaps."

"Dear me," she thought. "I have always told the boys that they need not do without things they couldn't buy; they could make them. But a lathe!"

She smiled across the table at her son, who was leaning on his elbows, looking at her hopefully. She hesitated before she repeated, "Perhaps. It won't be easy," she continued. "Anyway, I'll tell you all I remember about it. I'll make a sketch of your grandfather's lathe if you will get some paper."

Sterchens ran to watch her mother, and Will and Orv looked over her shoulder as she drew a neat picture of the lathe that she remembered in her father's shop.

The next day, in the barn loft, the boys began building their first machine. They decided to make the lathe eight feet long. It was to be run by a foot treadle. In their eagerness to have enough power, they did not follow their mother's sketch, but made the treadle much larger than it needed to be so that it was out of proportion to the rest of the machine.

All of the boys on their street were curious to see what was going on in the Wrights' barn. Her brothers let Sterchens watch while they worked, but they kept the big barn doors closed, and no one else was allowed to come in until the lathe was finished.

At last, Will and Orv were ready to try the machine, so they told their good friends, Edwin Sines and Johnny Murrow, that they could come and bring the gang to see it. When they started the lathe with the excited boys looking on, it made so much noise that not one of them realized a small cyclone had taken the skylight off the barn.

Sterchens started out to tell her mother the good news of the machine's success, but the force of the wind flattened her against the barn and held her there. Mother Wright looked out anxiously to see what was happening in the barn and was horrified to see her small daughter powerless in the storm. As she rushed to rescue her, the cyclone passed as quickly as it came. Mrs. Wright hugged Sterchens in frantic joy, saying over and over, "You're safe, my baby, you're safe."

But Sterchens, ignoring her recent danger, shouted over the noise of the receding storm the news she had come to tell: "It works, Mother, it works!"

Five: JOB PRINTERS

It had stopped snowing and settled down to a steady freeze. The ice on the pond near the high school was a clear, solid sheet, and the sky above was the same clear blue. Every boy in Dayton tingled with excitement. This was the day of the big ice hockey game, when the high school team would play the sons of army officers stationed at a fort nearby.

Will and Orv went to the pond together, talking about the game as they went. Orv was a good skater, even though he was too young to play. But Will was seventeen and one of the best skaters Dayton High had ever seen. Orv was very proud that his brother was on the team.

"You just show those army fellows a thing or two, Will," he said cockily, sure of his brother's skill. "I'll be waiting for you after the game."

But after the game, Orv walked home alone, his heart more lonely and frightened than it had ever been in his thirteen years. Will had been carried from the ice, badly injured. It happened in the sixth period. No one who watched the play during that breathless minute could know that the course of Will's life would change in those sixty seconds.

His injuries were very painful. Five of his teeth were knocked out, and severe infection set in. When three more teeth had to be removed, the shock was so great that Will was not able to return to school. He was so ill that he even had to give up his plan to enter Yale University in the autumn.

It was not easy for him to give up his dream. Will wanted to be a teacher, and he kept hoping that he could go to college. But it was several years before he felt well again, and he decided that he had been away from his studies too long. He never went back to school after that game.

Orv missed Will's companionship very much while his brother was ill. He kept thinking of things they could do, of things they could make on the lathe. But when he dashed upstairs to their bedroom to share the ideas which so thrilled him, Will was too ill to do more than nod and say listlessly, "That sounds fine, Orvie."

As time passed and his brother still was not well enough to join in his schemes, the ever-active Orv started a printing business with his friend Edwin Sines as a partner. Ed, who lived two houses down the street, had one dollar to invest in some enterprise, and Orv convinced him that this was a good place for it.

But first, Orv asked Will if he would care. He sat on the edge of his brother's bed.

"Of course, Will, it won't be the same—not fun like our doing things together," he said as he twisted a corner of the patchwork quilt. "You know that. But Ed has a dollar to put in, and Mrs. Sines says we can use her kitchen for a shop. Father knows where he can get some secondhand type for us real cheap."

"Sure, Orv, that's all right. Go ahead. Soon as I get out of here I'll help you and Ed." He gave his brother's hand an affectionate pat and smiled as Orv ran down the stairs.

Orv and his partner were in the eighth grade. Although they felt sure that they were capable of any sort of printing, they decided to start by publishing a school paper. They called it the Midget and announced that subscriptions might be paid in popcorn and candy if no cash was available. This was a mistake and led to many arguments.

"Buzz Johnson says he subscribed to the Midget last week, and he didn't get a paper. Paid candy for it, he says," Orv stormed into the Sines kitchen. "I told him I never saw it." Seeing Ed's sheepish look, Orv stopped. "Not again! You didn't eat another subscription?" he asked indignantly.

Ed was always hungry after school. But this was a matter of principle as well as of hunger with him. He thought that whatever was taken in belonged to the partners. Orv thought they should sell the candy and add the money to their capital. Since they could not agree, Orv offered to buy Ed's interest in the business for one dollar, the amount of his investment. Then he hired Ed to work for wages.

Now that he was the sole owner of a printing business, Orv decided to build a real press. Dusting off the old lathe in the barn, he began shaping sticks of wood for the frame. From his old friend the junk dealer, he bought a metal roller that he filled with gravel to give it weight.

Once more Sterchens was allowed to watch as a new machine was tried. She bent over eagerly while Orv inked the type, set a piece of paper on it, and ran the roller. Anxiously, she watched as he lifted the sheet. It worked! She could see the words on the paper!

"Here, Sterchens, show this to Will," Orv said proudly, handing the sheet to his sister. "Hold it out—like this—so the ink won't smudge."

Although she wanted to run with the good news, Sterchens walked into the living room, holding the paper out stiffly, and laid it on the couch where Will was resting. But she could not keep the excitement from her voice while she announced with pride as great as Orv's own, "It works! See, it works!"

When Will was able to "putter around" as he called it, he added a lever to the press the younger boy had built. This lever shot the roller back and forth, so there was no need to walk and push it.

At last, the brothers could work together again. The next thing they made was a machine to fold copies of the church paper, which Father Wright edited. Like the lathe, it made a great deal of noise and shook the walls of the little shop they had fixed up in the barn. But unlike the lathe, it did work. The boys were free from the long task of folding the papers by hand. They whistled and sang at the top of their lungs as the folded papers dropped from the clattering machine. Their father paid them two dollars a week for folding the papers, so Will and Orv thought this was an easy way to earn money.

"Pretty soft job, Orvie," Will shouted above the din.

"Sure is, now we have the machine," Orv shouted in reply as he stacked the papers.

They were so busy with their new machine that they did not notice Father Wright as he watched them from the door. He shook his head as he turned away, saying to himself, "Those boys, what will they make next?"

A chance came to add to Orv's small stock of type at a bargain. It was a great temptation.

"Let's take it, Will, and set up as printers," Orv urged. "We could print a paper with news of this neighborhood and get the storekeepers to pay for advertising. We could even strike off business cards and posters if people wanted them."

"We'd have to have a shop, Orv, to do the job right," Will reasoned. "With a sign. Can't you just see it?"

"Wright and Wright, Printers," Orv's mind leaped ahead, and his eyes shone as they looked into the future. "'Wright and Wright, Job Printers.' That might bring in more work."

Their mother heard the boys talking about the shop. More than anything in the world she wanted to make their dream come true. She did not have much, but what she had was theirs. She insisted that Will and Orv take it all and open a shop. How happy they were when she told them her plan!

"You and Sterchens will be partners, too. The shop will belong to us all," Will said affectionately.

The boys rented a small room in a brick building on West Third Street. It seemed just right for a shop.

On the day the sign went up, March 1, 1889, it read as Orv had planned:

WRIGHT AND WRIGHT, JOB PRINTERS

It was quite a large sign for a small shop. It was a large sign, indeed, for two young printers, twenty-one and seventeen. Mother Wright smiled when she saw it.

The boys had insisted that she and Sterchens come to inspect the shop, for they wanted to surprise them. First, they showed them the shelves they had made to hold their boxes of supplies. Then, from the press in the middle of the floor they drew out with a flourish the first issue of the West Side News.

Mother Wright read the opening words, "This week we issue the first number of the West Side News, a paper to be published in the interests of the people and the business institutions  of the West Side. Whatever tends to their advancement—moral, mental, and financial—will receive our closest attention."

Then she turned through the little four-page paper. Here was a news item about the inauguration of the new President, Benjamin Harrison; here was a story about Abraham Lincoln and General Sherman; here was an article about Benjamin Franklin.

Will and Orv watched her closely as she examined their paper. "What do you think of it, Mother? Do you like it?" they exclaimed together.

Mother Wright looked at her sons. "How tall they have grown," she thought. "And now they are in business for themselves. I'm glad I could see them here."

"Yes, boys, I like it. I think it's wonderful, just wonderful. I'm so proud of you."

Suddenly, she felt tired. "Come, Sterchens, we must go now." She did not want to mar the happiness of her sons by saying she was ill. She even managed a joke as she left, "These business men will be hungry; we must have supper ready for them."

For several years, Mother Wright had been growing weaker. She had worked hard while her children were small, carrying the full responsibility of the home while her husband was away on long trips for his church. Often short of money and having only the simplest housekeeping equipment, she never spared herself, so that her family did not lack anything they really needed. Now she must rest often.

She lived only four months after the shop was opened. But she read every word in the West Side News and saw that whatever tended to the advancement of the community was, indeed, receiving their closest attention, as the young editors had promised in the first issue. She saw reflected there the influence of the books the family had read together. She saw the interest in other lands and peoples that she had fostered. Most clearly, she saw reflected the whole spirit of their home.

For her father's wish on her wedding day had come true. Susan Koerner Wright had truly known how to make a happy home.

Six: Sterchens Grows Up

For fifteen years she had been Sterchens, the much loved little sister, adored and protected by everyone in the Wright home. Now Sterchens must grow up. Now she must be Katharine and mistress of this home. She must try to take her mother's place.

Everywhere she looked there was something to remind her—her mother's apron still hanging on the hook, the tea towels she had lately hemmed, the potholders she had made from scraps of her old dresses.

Father Wright could find refuge in his study upstairs. There, among his books, he found solace in thinking of his wife, in the remembrance of the devotion they had shared during their years together.

Wilbur and Orville could silently put on their caps and walk together to their shop, where they worked long hours, each hesitating to speak of their loss lest he add to the sorrow of the other.

For Katharine there was no such comfort. Here, surrounded by all the familiar things that seemed to speak of her mother's love and care, she must face her grief alone.

She was glad when it was time for school to begin in September. Of course, it meant that she was busy every minute of the day, with housekeeping before and after school hours. But it meant also that there was less time for grieving.

As Thanksgiving approached, Katharine planned a surprise for her brothers. Although in most matters they agreed perfectly, each had his favorite pie. Mother Wright always baked two kinds of pie on holidays, pumpkin pie for Wilbur and mincemeat pie for Orville. Katharine had resolved to do everything her mother would have done.

She tried to roll the dough into the flaky, thin crust, which had made her mother's pies so delicious. But the dough stuck to the rolling pin and would not stay in place. She struggled again and again to shape it to the tins. She did not know whether her fillings

were too thick or too thin. But, at last, the pies were
in the oven.

When the weary girl brought them to the table,
her brothers could not bear even to try them. They
missed their mother so. Katharine looked anxiously
from one to the other. She saw the look of pain in
Orville's eyes. She saw Wilbur pick up his fork, then
slowly put it down.

"I've tried, I've really tried," Katharine sobbed as
she left the table and went to her room.

At a nod from their father, her brothers followed
her, to comfort her if they could. Suddenly they realized how hard the past weeks had been for her.

"We've been selfish, Sterchens," Wilbur said sadly.
"We just thought of ourselves and of how much we
missed Mother. We should have known that all the
time you were missing her most of all."

After this, they often asked Katharine to help them
in the shop by setting type, and in the evenings they
all sat together in the living room once more. Because
Bishop Wright's duties frequently took him far from
Dayton and his eldest sons, Reuchlin and Lorin, had
married and were living in homes of their own, Will
and Orv and Sterchens were often alone in the house
at 7 Hawthorne Street.

While their sister studied her lessons for the next
day, the boys read or sketched. They found themselves turning to her for advice as they had to their
mother.

"Sterchens reminds me of Mother, more every day," Wilbur said thoughtfully when he and his brother were alone.

"And she doesn't look like Mother at all," Orville added. "She just is like Mother."

The three shared the sorrow that had now come to their house as they had shared its joys in the past. In this sharing, they were bound together by ties of loyalty and affection, which nothing in their future lives could ever break.

So Sterchens grew up. And in spite of the fact that, as long as they lived, their youthful spirits made Will and Orv known in Dayton as the "Wright boys," they did some growing up, too.

They worked hard to improve the West Side News. Beginning with one hundred subscribers, they soon had to hire two boys to deliver the papers to three hundred Dayton homes. For a year, Orville had been taking special courses in Latin and other required subjects so that he might enter college. But he became so interested in the printing business and in doing things with Wilbur that he decided not to go.

"Tell you what, Will," he said one evening. "Let's change the paper to a daily."

"Seems to me it's hard enough for us to get out a weekly, with all the other things we do," Will answered in surprise. "It takes a lot of time to set the type by hand and fuss over the press when it breaks down, besides checking up on subscriptions."

"I know it does, Will, but I've decided not to go to college. I'm sure we can swing it."

The new daily was called The Evening Item, and publishing it did not leave much time for the "other things" of which Will spoke. Chief of these was tinkering with their own bikes and those of their friends.

When the craze for bicycling that swept across the country struck Dayton, some young people were given expensive models by their families. But there was no money in the Wright house to be spent in this way. So once more Will and Orv set about making what they could not buy. They put together parts of several old machines and made bicycles that ran along at almost racing speed.

There were very few bicycle repair shops anywhere, so the boys were constantly asked to fix the broken machines of Edwin Sines, Chauncey Smith, and other friends. While they were very glad to do this, it was often difficult, even for such clever mechanics as Will and Orv had become. What they really needed was a supply of parts to replace what was missing or broken. So, Wright and Wright, Job Printers, added a bicycle repair department.

Soon the little shop was so crowded with bicycles to be repaired that they stopped publishing their newspaper and hired Ed Sines to look after the job printing for them. Meanwhile, they rented a shop across the street. Now there were two signs facing each other on West Third Street: Wright and Wright, Job Printers, and Wright Cycle Co.

Ed Sines put on his printer's apron and got ready for business. "Will and Orv are good friends," he thought. "I'm glad they're making a success."

Most people in Dayton owned the old-fashioned kind of bicycles, with a large front wheel and a small one at the back. There were no brakes, and the tires were solid.

In 1892, there was a new, European-type bicycle on the market, and Will and Orv each bought one with money they had saved from their work in the printing shop. The wheels, front and back, were the same size. The rubber tires were not solid, but were pumped up with air, so it was like riding on cushions after bumping over the rough roads on their old bicycles.

"Everybody will want one," the boys agreed, and so they arranged to have several makes of the new-style machines for sale in the Wright Cycle Co. shop when bicycling weather came in the spring.

It seemed that nearly everybody did want one. Twice the Wright Cycle Co. had to move to larger quarters. Will and Orv were so busy that they decided to close the printing shop and devote all of their time to the bicycle business.

But they were not satisfied just to sell machines and repair them when something went wrong. They wanted to be making them. They always wanted to be making something. Then, too, they felt that most bicycles were not really safe. They were sure they could build one that would be safer.

So the following year they began putting together the model of a ball-bearing safety machine they had

been talking about for a long time. All of the bicycles manufactured by big firms in the East had names, so they named their new bicycle the "Van Cleve" after one of their ancestors, Catharine Van Cleve, one of the first settlers of Dayton.

The demand for the Van Cleve bicycle with its safety brake was so great that Will and Orv had to spend all of their time making them. They engaged a helper to look after repair jobs, while they worked on the new machines from early in the morning until ten o'clock at night.

Katharine had gone away to college, to Oberlin College in Ohio. All winter her brothers talked about what they could do to make her happy when she came home for the summer vacation.

Will was the one who first thought of the wonderful surprise that they planned for her.

"We could put a porch on the front of the house," he said one day in early spring. "She'll want to have some of her new friends from college come to visit.

The porch would be a nice place for them to sit in the evening."

"Let's get going," Orv replied. "Why didn't we think of it before?"

So they hurried to add a porch to the old frame house before their sister came home.

But when summer came, she had no time to enjoy the porch. For Orville was very ill with typhoid fever. The doctor wanted to bring a nurse, but Katharine insisted on caring for her brother during the day. At night, Wilbur took his turn keeping cold cloths on Orville's forehead and waiting for the fever to go down.

When Orville had been unconscious for nearly two weeks, Katharine said to the doctor in a shaking voice, "Is he going to get well, doctor? He's just nothing but skin and bones."

The doctor looked from Orville to his sister and brother, their faces drawn with anxiety and loss of sleep, and said, "Skin and bones goes for the three of you, I'd say. I can't make any promises in a case like this, but I do know if good care means anything he will get well."

Eventually, Orville did get well, but it was a very slow and patience-trying process for him and his family. Orville had been well and active during all of his twenty-five years. It was difficult for him to stay in bed when there were so many things he wanted to do. Ridiculous! But when he tried to get up, he stumbled and fell against the bed. "Maybe the doctor is right," he thought, as he leaned back weakly against the pillows.

Katharine made cup custards and apple snow and all the strength-giving foods that the invalid was allowed to have.

When Orville began to feel better, he was very restless. Wilbur read to him by the hour so he would rest in bed.

One day he read an article that told of the death of the German, Otto Lilienthal, who was called the "Father of Gliding Flights." For twenty-five years he had been trying to fly. He made some flights, gliding a little way from a hillside, then falling, and trying to discover why he could not stay up. Now he had fallen for the last time.

When Wilbur finished reading, Orville said quietly, "Will, does that make you think of anything?"

His brother hesitated. Then he smiled down at Orv. "The helicopter."

"Maybe there's something in this flying business," said Orv, his eyes lighted up. "Something big."

Wilbur watched his brother's dull, sickly face take on that eager look once again, and Wilbur's heart swelled. That was enough for him. "Let's find out," he said. "I'll get some books."

Seven: A New Hobby

And so the Wrights were off on another hobby. Will dashed off a letter to the Smithsonian Institution in Washington, asking for a list of books on gliding. The secretary told him to order Progress in Flying by Octave Chanute and a book by Professor Langley, Director of the Smithsonian. He promised to send free of charge some pamphlets that the Institution had published.

Orv was so eager to learn about their new hobby that he got very restless lying in bed, waiting for these books to come. So Will went to the public library and brought home everything he could find about men who had tried to fly. He piled the books and magazines on his brother's bed.

"There now, these ought to keep you busy for a while."

All of the books looked interesting. Orv could not decide which to read first. But the doctor decided for him. He was to read none of them. Orv was propped up on his pillows with one of the books in his hand when the doctor came for his daily visit.

"Katharine, take these books away," he called sternly. "Your brother is still too weak to read." Then, seeing how much better his patient looked, he asked curiously, "What kind of a book is it? What's it about?"

With a flash of his old enthusiasm, Orv replied, "Experiments in flying. Will and I thought we would read up on the subject."

"Humph—flying, indeed! You'd better get strong enough to walk before you start to fly. Of all the foolish ways for two grown men to waste their time! I am surprised at Will."

When Katharine reported this conversation to Will, he was disturbed. "Maybe it is foolish," he thought. "The doctor is right—we are grown men. Orv was twenty-five his last birthday, and I am twenty-nine." Then he remembered the look on his brother's face when he saw the books. "Why, he looked just like a boy," he said to himself, "and I felt like one. Anything that makes you that happy can't be foolish." And Will went up the stairs two steps at a time.

"The doctor says I can't read any more," Orv said sadly, as Will came in his room.

"I know. Sterchens told me. But he didn't say anything about my reading to you, did he?" his brother inquired.

Every afternoon, Will hurried home from the shop to read to Orv. They already knew about Lilienthal and his man-carrying kite. Now they learned that men in other countries had tried to fly. In England, Hiram Maxim and the engineer Pilcher, Ader in France, and Octave Chanute in the United States had all experimented with gliders. But no one was trying now. Lilienthal and Pilcher had been killed; the others had quit.

The night before Katharine went back to college in September, Orville was able to come downstairs. To celebrate the event, his father brought an old book from his study and gave it to Orv.

"Here, Son, you may find something interesting in this. It is called Animal Mechanism, and there is a section on flight. Bird flight, that is," he added with a chuckle.

"Thanks very much, Father. Will and I will read it. Any kind of flight interests us."

Soon the brothers were alone, for Father Wright's duties called him to the Pacific Coast. They took turns reading aloud in the long evenings, and they talked and dreamed over what they read.

Will wrote to Octave Chanute in Chicago and told him that he and his brother had read his book. Did he know of any others? He replied that there were very few books about gliding but that some articles had been printed in scientific magazines. He sent them a list. This kind act was the beginning of a friendship between Chanute and the Wrights which was to last as long as they lived.

Will and Orv kept on reading. And the more they read, the more surprised they were. Not one of the men they read about seemed to have solved the problem of keeping his balance in the air. That was it—you must keep your balance. Then the glider would not fall.

When the spring of 1900 came, their minds were made up. They would not read or talk about it any longer. They would build a glider and see for themselves why the others had failed. Lilienthal and Chanute had shifted their bodies from side to side to balance their gliders in the air. A better way than that must be found.

Although the bicycle shop was a very busy place that summer, Will and Orv thought about their glider whenever they had any free time. How could they make it balance in the air? They had read Father Wright's book about birds carefully. Perhaps if they watched birds flying they might get an idea.

Every Sunday, when the weather was fair, they rode their bicycles to the hill where they had flown kites when they were children. Here they lay on the grass and watched the long flight of large hawks and buzzards as they soared overhead. On weekdays, from the windows of their shop, they watched the quick, short flights of swallows and small birds.

But for all their watching, it was not from birds that the Wrights learned the secret of balance in the air. It was from a pasteboard box!

When the two brothers first began talking about a glider, Orv suggested that the wings should be hinged so they could be moved up and down to secure lateral control. Even though he and Wilbur thought and thought, they could not find any way to manage it.

Then one night in the bicycle shop, when Wilbur must still have been thinking about the problem, he opened a pasteboard box to show a rubber tube to a customer. The man took a long time to decide whether or not he would buy it. As he stood waiting, Wilbur twisted the corners of the box in opposite directions with his long, muscular fingers. Looking down, he saw that his fingers had solved the problem; not hinged wings, but ones which could be twisted. He could scarcely wait for the man to go. Closing the shop, he rushed home with the box in his hands. He must tell Orville.

But his brother was not at home. He had gone to a concert with Katharine. Wilbur sat under the gas lamp in the living room, twisting the corners of the box again and again. And with every twist he became more confident that this was the answer to the problem of balance in the air.

It was midnight before Katharine and Orville came home. The usually calm Will was so excited they could not imagine what had happened.

He showed them the box. Orv caught the idea at once, and then his eyes shone with excitement, too. The brothers both talked at once, explaining it to Katharine. She looked at the box and tried her best to understand, but she finally gave up and went to bed—happy because Will and Orv would be happy now. The question that had worried them so long seemed settled.

"We'd better try a model first," Wilbur said cautiously the next morning.

"Yes, then if it doesn't work, we won't be out anything. No use to build a big machine until we're sure." For a change, Orville was cautious this time, too.

The model they made was five feet from tip to tip and looked like a box kite.

On the first windy day after it was finished, Will took the model to the hill and threw it into the air. He held the strings that were fastened to the corners and guided the kite by twisting them in his hands. A crowd of small boys followed him. It was not a common thing to see a man fly a kite. This was not a common kite, either. They jumped about and yelled as it flew from one side to the other, controlled by the strings in Will's hands.

"Some kite you got there, Mister," one of them exclaimed admiringly.

"Yes, sonny, some kite," Will said happily, as he pulled it in.

The boys started home to supper, still talking about the strange kite they had seen.

When Will reached home, Orv was just coming in. He had stayed at the shop to wait on customers.

"How did it go, Will?" he asked anxiously.

One look at her brother's smiling face told Katharine that she did not need to ask.

"It works," she stated.

Will nodded in satisfaction.

Now they could build the glider.

Wilbur asked Katharine to let him use her sewing machine. How the neighbors stared when he and Orv carried it to the backyard and set it up on the green lawn! Here he sat sewing yards and yards of cream-colored sateen. Meanwhile, in the workroom in back of the bicycle shop, Orville shaped pieces of tough, elastic wood from an ash tree for the frame.

At last, the sewing machine was carried back into the house. The shop was closed.

For a few days, there was confusion in the house on Hawthorne Street. The living room floor was covered with boxes of piano wire, screws, rolls of bicycle tape, and billowing yards of sateen.

Katharine could scarcely find a place to step. She did not even try to dust.

"Such a racket," she said, putting her hands over her ears.

Then, suddenly, the house was quiet. The boxes and packages were gone. Her brothers were gone. Katharine was so lonely that she wished she could have all the confusion and the racket back again.

Will had been too busy to notice the neighbors who watched him from their windows as he sewed. But Katharine had seen them. She knew they had not hesitated to say how silly it looked to see a man sewing in the backyard. The neighbors were more curious than ever now that Will and Orv were gone.

They quizzed Katharine, but all she would say was that her brothers had gone on a vacation. When they asked where, she only smiled. She was not sure herself. She could not even find Kitty Hawk on the map.

Eight: THE WIND

This hard-to-find Kitty Hawk was a fishing village on a lonely strip of sand off the coast of North Carolina. On the ocean side, the wind blew straight from the Atlantic. On the landward side, stormy gales swept in from three great sounds, Albemarle, Roanoke, and Pamlico. Here, surrounded by water and the wind, was Kitty Hawk. Twenty houses, widely scattered, with a lifesaving station, weather bureau, and post office, made up the little settlement.

Because it was lonely, Wilbur and Orville thought it would be just the place to try

their glider. For one thing, there would be no one to laugh at them or bother them. But that was not the real reason they chose Kitty Hawk. They chose it because of the wind. When they wrote to the Weather Bureau in Washington asking where the wind was strongest and steadiest, the answer was, "at Kitty Hawk."

"That's the spot for us, then," Will said. He started a few days before Orv, so he could look for a good place to camp.

Kitty Hawk was not only hard to find on Katharine's map; when Wilbur reached Elizabeth City, North Carolina, the end of his train journey, he met no one at first who had even heard of Kitty Hawk. At the ticket office in Dayton, he had been told that he must go part of the way by boat. So he walked to the waterfront. Here he learned that a boat departed once a week for Roanoke Island, six miles from Kitty Hawk. But it had gone the day before. Will felt numb with fatigue and discouragement.

At this point, all he noticed was a dirty little schooner tied up at the wharf.

The captain of the schooner introduced himself. "My name's Perry. Where did you want to go, Mister?"

"Kitty Hawk," Will replied grimly. "Ever hear of it?"

"Kitty Hawk? You don't say!" Captain Perry's amazement was plain. "I ought to know where it is. I used to live there, myself. This is my boat. I'll take you."

Will hesitated. He looked out over the choppy waters of the long, broad inlet of the ocean. The boat was small and dingy. It did not look as if it would hold together in a storm. But he could not wait a week.

"As soon as I get my stuff from the station," he said, "we can start."

The captain was curious about his passenger. He did not know when he had seen a stranger in Kitty Hawk. "Why is this fellow in such a hurry to get there?" he wondered.

He was even more curious when he saw Will and a station porter come staggering down the street with the tent and heavy packages of glider parts. But he helped load them on the deck and hurried to get under way. Time for questions would come later, for now a strong wind was beginning to blow.

After a few miles, the wind was so strong that the captain was afraid to head into Albemarle Sound. He dropped anchor and waited a day before he felt it was safe to go on.

"We picked the right place for wind," Will said to himself as he hung onto the railing of the tossing boat. Instead of a voyage of a few hours, he spent two days and nights on board the old schooner.

Captain Perry cooked hearty meals for himself in the tiny galley and asked Will to share them. But both galley and food looked so dirty that Will declined. The captain was sympathetic. He thought his passenger was seasick!

For forty-eight hours, the only thing Will had to eat was a glass of jelly that Katharine had slipped in his suitcase as he was leaving.

On reaching Kitty Hawk, Wilbur's first thought was to find a place to live until Orville came. The William Tates had a spare bedroom. As soon as they saw Will, they liked him and said he could stay with them as long as he wanted to. How he enjoyed Mrs. Tate's good meals after his diet of jelly!

Mrs. Tate was in charge of the little Kitty Hawk post office. Her husband had held this position for so many years before she took his place that everyone in the village still called him "Postmaster Tate."

The spot Will picked for a camp was about half a mile from the Tates' home. There were a few trees, so Will tied the tent to one of them. His next job was to bring the boxes of tools and glider materials to the camp. The boxes were heavy at the start, and they got heavier each foot of the half mile. Will had come from a cool city of gardens and green lawns. He was almost blinded by the glare of the sun as it beat down upon the white sand. He had to stop every few minutes to wipe the perspiration from his face. His shirt was soon wet through and sticking to his back. If only Orv had come with him! Will missed his brother's help, but even more, he missed his cheerful whistle.

He smiled when he remembered that his brother had insisted upon packing his mandolin. Orv thought he was coming on a vacation. "Well, it hasn't been much of a vacation so far," Will thought, as he slapped at a sand flea. "But let him bring it. Maybe a mandolin will be just what we need."

When Orv arrived, the brothers started living in their camp. Orv said he would not mind doing the cooking, and he soon got their little gasoline stove going. Will said he would not mind doing the dishes. Each time they came to Kitty Hawk they divided the work in this way. Each one was happy and was sure he had the best of the bargain. Will did not complain because he had to carry all of the water a thousand feet, for Orv had his troubles, too. They had no milk, and there was no place to buy bread. Orv said that did not matter, he would just bake biscuits—bake hot biscuits three times a day! But he soon worked out an easy way to do it. He mixed enough flour and baking powder with shortening to last several days, then all he had to do was rush in at mealtime and stir up a batch with water. Orv was proud of his bis-cuit-mix idea, for it helped him save time for work on the glider.

Food did not matter much, anyway. After Will and Orv started building the glider, they could scarcely stop long enough to eat or sleep. They could not even wait until the machine was finished to try it out from the top of a sand dune. Tying a rope to its nose, they let the wind take it. When it rose into the air and pulled on the rope with the strength of a wild horse, they were beside themselves with joy.

"It works, Will, it works!" Orv shouted into the gale.

The wind carried his voice away, and Will could not hear him, so he called out, too, "It works, it really works!" as he tugged at the rope.

Now they must try to ride this plunging creature. It was time to test it as a glider, not as a huge kite.

This meant that they must carry it four miles from their camp to the top of the largest sand dune. There were many of these mounds on that part of the coast, but here the winds had piled the sand up and up until the dune was so large that it was called a hill, Kill Devil Hill, one hundred feet high.

Postmaster Tate came to watch them. Also, some of the coast guards from the Kitty Hawk station came. They helped start the glider from the top of the dune.

One after the other, Will and Orv stretched out, face downward in the center of the glider. They hooked their feet over a bar at the back to brace themselves. With their hands, they grasped a bar in front that moved the rudder.

"Ready!" The men pulled the kite down the hill by its rope. When it gained speed, it rose with its passenger in the air! After a few feet, the kite dropped. They tried again and then again.

"How does it feel, boys?" Mr. Tate wanted to know when Will and Orv were ready to stop.

"My heart was up between my shoulders," answered Will.

"My lower jaw was where the upper one should be," said Orv, shaking his head to see if it was still in place after the jolts of his first ride in a glider.

In the days that followed, the Wrights put the glider through dozens of tests. Sometimes it was eight feet from the ground, sometimes only five. But these tests proved the thing they had come to Kitty Hawk to learn. They had found that the way to keep a glider balanced in the air was to make the air itself balance the machine as it tipped from side to side.

When the tests were finished, it was late in October, long past time for vacations to end. Will and Orv must go home and open the bicycle shop again if they were to have money enough to come back to Kitty Hawk the next summer. Now they were sure this was what they wanted to do.

"What shall we do with the glider?" asked Wilbur as they packed their tools.

"Just let it blow away, I guess," Orville replied. "We'll have to build a new one next year, anyway; a larger one, maybe," he added.

So the last thing before they left, the brothers climbed to the top of Kill Devil Hill, carrying their glider. They thought the winter winds would carry it into the Atlantic.

But after the Wrights had gone, Mr. Tate decided the glider might still be of some use. He dragged it home and chopped up the framework for firewood. When his wife saw that the wide sateen wings were not torn, she was happy.

"Just the thing, to make dresses for the two girls," she said. So the little Tate girls had new dresses that winter. They looked so pretty in them that no one ever dreamed they were wearing part of a glider.

Katharine was a teacher now, teaching Latin in her old high school. She was so busy that winter when she came home after school, with the house to keep and papers to grade, that she did not realize how many evenings Will and Orv spent talking about their experiments at Kitty Hawk.

On one of the first warm days of spring, Wilbur walked into the kitchen while she was getting breakfast ready. "May I borrow your sewing machine again, Katharine?" he asked.

She caught her breath. What did this mean? Were her brothers planning to go away again, leaving her alone for the summer? A summer of questions, of sly jokes about the Wright boys and their "kite" as the neighbors called it?

But she knew how much this hobby meant to them. They worked so hard and had so little fun. She would not object.

"Of course, Will, use the machine any time you want it," she replied as she continued her tasks in the kitchen.

Once more the sewing machine was carried out onto the lawn. The material that Wilbur used this time was heavy muslin instead of sateen. He and Orv planned to build a larger glider, and they figured it might be a good thing to have really strong cloth to cover the wings.

This year they knew how to prepare for camp life. Orv did not pack his mandolin; he knew he would be too busy to play. But he and Will packed many tins of fruit and vegetables that Katharine had put up, as well as their tools and materials. For they intended to build a shed near Kill Devil Hill, so they could work on the glider near the spot where it would be tested. They could be more comfortable in the tent if it did not have to shelter both them and the glider.

Her brothers were so excited over their plans that they said good-bye to Katharine in July and left for Kitty Hawk. They could not wait any longer to try out the ideas they had talked about all winter.

But the glider they built this year was a disappointment. In spite of heavier cloth for the wings and changes in the frame, this larger machine did not fly as well as they had hoped.

Octave Chanute paid a short visit to the camp and urged them to continue their experiments. He told them that he was sure they had already broken the records for speed and distance in gliding.

But control and balance, not speed and distance, were the things for which they were working. And they had not been able to control the glider in the air as they had planned.

They wanted to quit. But they did not. Day after day they went over every part of the glider, trying to find where they had made a mistake in its design.

As they worked beside the great dune in the blazing sun, the gulls which circled and dipped above them seemed to be screaming in derision, "Why do you try, why do you try? Only a bird can fly!"

When darkness forced them back to their tent and they lay on their cots, sunburned and stiff, the wind seemed to be trying to push the tent down—to sweep them away and prove that the wind and the air would never know a master.

At last, Will and Orv agreed that what they had suspected the year before must be true. The printed tables showing the lift and drag of the wind were not correct. What could two bicycle mechanics do without accurate tables to use?

"I know what we can do," Orv said bitterly, as he threw down his tools. "We can go back to the bicycle shop."

"Yes." Will started packing. "And this time we will stay."

They had been too disheartened to write to their sister. When they reached home, Katharine was eager to hear about what they had done.

Orv's report was a short one. "This time it didn't work."

Will shook his head in complete dejection as he said, "Man won't be flying for a thousand years."

NINE: THE TUNNEL

Will and Orv scarcely had time to catch up with their work in the shop when a letter came from Chicago. This was one of the most important letters ever written in this country. At the time, it did not look as if it were important to anyone except Wilbur, because it was an invitation for him to speak before the Western Society of Engineers. It was signed by Octave Chanute, who was president of the society. But the letter was important to everyone, for it speeded the invention of the airplane by no one can guess how many years.

Will was surprised, and he made up his mind right away that he would not go. When he showed the invitation to his brother and sister, they were surprised, too, but delighted.

"Oh, Will, how wonderful!" Katharine cried. "You must accept."

Flatly, Will said, "No, I can't go. Even if I wanted to, there isn't time to make up a speech. The meeting is September eighteenth and here it is the last of August. No, I can't do it," he repeated firmly.

Katharine was crushed.

"But, Will, it's such an honor!" she protested. "You have never been asked to speak right here in Dayton. Now you're invited to address a meeting where there will be people from all over this part of the country."

"That's just it," Will said, already cold with fright at the prospect. "I never have made a speech. I never want to make one. I'm not a public speaker. I'm just a bicycle mechanic."

Orville joined the argument.

"Of course, I hate to see you turn down Chanute," he said slowly. "He is the only one beside Katharine and Father who showed any interest in our gliding."

"He went clear to Kitty Hawk this summer," Katharine reminded him. "Don't forget that."

She did so want Will to go. "I guess that would show the folks in Dayton what people away from home think of the Wright boys and their kites," she thought fiercely to herself.

Reluctantly, Will agreed with Katharine and Orville that he could not refuse Chanute. But he wrote Chanute that he would not come if any announcement was made about his speech or if he had to wear a dress suit—he did not have one. What could he speak about, anyway, to these men who had built railroads and bridges all over the world. All he had ever built were bicycles in Dayton and, of course, for fun, two gliders.

Octave Chanute smiled when he received the letter. He intended to announce the speech, anyway, and the dress suit did not matter. But he did tell Will what he could talk about. Some Aeronautical Experiments would be a good subject, he wrote.

When Will told his brother some of the things he was going to say, Orv was scared. Will said he was going to say that there were many mistakes in the figures on air pressure in the scientific books. The mistakes about the pressure of air on curved surfaces were especially bad.

The more Orv thought about it, the more scared he was. He could just see Will standing there before a big roomful of dressed-up men who had all gone to college, telling them that the books they had studied were wrong. He could not bear it if they laughed at his brother. What if he and Will were the ones who were wrong? After all, as Will had said, they were just bicycle mechanics.

Well, there was one way to find out. While Will worked on his speech, Orv rigged up a little wind tunnel out of a box he found in the shop. He put a glass top on it and hung a few curved and a few flat pieces of cardboard on a metal rod inside. Then he waited to see what happened to them when a blast of air was forced through the box.

Although there was not time to make as many tests as he wished, it took just one day to convince Orv that he and Will were the ones who were right.

The engineers did not laugh at Will. In fact, they thought his speech was so important that they asked him to let them publish it in their official magazine, the Journal of the Western Society of Engineers.

Will and Orv had been so discouraged when they left Kitty Hawk that they had intended to give all of their time to the bicycle business. Not ever again would they think about building a glider. But if they were to be asked to speak before societies of learned men and even to have what they said printed, they'd better be sure just how right they were and how wrong the other fellows were.

The wind tunnel that Orv had made in such a great hurry was only a foot and a half long. He and Will now decided to build one six feet long so they could make more tests. After all, if they should change their minds and decide to continue gliding, they could not afford to keep on building gliders just to see how they would act in the air. They would have to know, before they spent any more money on their hobby.

For the Wrights still thought of gliding as a hobby. They did not dream that with Will's speech in Chicago and Orv's eighteen-inch wind tunnel, they had started on a new path—a path that would lead them to a place beside the greatest scientists in the history of the world. But both Will and Orv did realize that they could do very little more until they had correct tables of air pressure. They must know what happened when the wind struck a flat object, and what was the difference in its force when the surface was curved.

Just as they had made their own lathe and printing press when they were children, so now they set about making their own air tables.

Scholars in France and England had spent many thousands of dollars making the air tables, which were not accurate. Tables that were right were made by Wilbur and Orville at a cost of fifteen dollars. Instead of going to a great deal of trouble to move an object through the air, in their tunnel they moved air on the object. The wind was made by an old fan, run by a small gas engine they used in their shop.

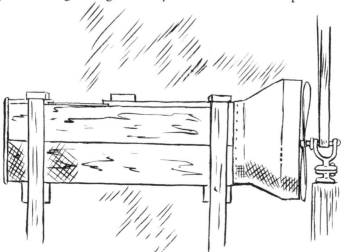

This box was quite different from the great tunnels of glass and steel that are built today by governments and by airplane factories. But here the Wrights tested more than two hundred small wings of different shapes and materials. Here, in the winter months, while there was not much business in the bicycle shop, they discovered principles that are used today whenever a plane is built.

The few customers who came in had to look for the brothers in the room back of their shop. They gazed at the wind tunnel in amazement.

"What's that contraption got to do with building bicycles? Just tell me that," one of them exclaimed.

"The only thing that contraption has to do with building bicycles," Orv answered, winking at Will, "is that bicycles paid for it."

Katharine gave up trying to serve meals at the usual hours. She never knew when her brothers would remember to come home. She kept food hot for them on the back of the stove.

Hour after hour, they watched as the air blew through their improvised wind tunnel. Their eyes ached. Hours stretched to weary days and then to weeks.

But the Wrights were learning the effects of the airflow by taking extremely accurate measurements of the acting forces.

As they studied the effects of the flow on the model wings, ideas moved like the wind across their minds.

When they were sure that they had watched long enough, they took a large sheet of wrapping paper and set down on it the figures that ultimately made it possible for men to fly.

Now they had to test these figures with larger wings. For the third time, Katharine's sewing machine was moved out. Again Will covered the lawn with pieces of muslin.

As Katharine sat by the window grading Latin papers, she could hear Will's whistle above the whirr of the machine. Fondly, she shook her head. Would they never really grow up, these brothers of hers? For three years she had heard little beside gliders and air tables talked about. Now they were planning to build a new glider with a tail like a fin. Where would this hobby lead them?

When Will and Orv reached Kitty Hawk, they found that the winter storms had battered their camp. The shed had to be repaired. They decided to make it larger while they were about it, so that they could live as well as work there. In a few days, they were ready to assemble their new glider with a tail.

Although, at times, the tail seemed to steady the machine, at other times it seemed to hinder its flight. Will and Orv were completely puzzled when the glider they had planned with such care came near to crashing several times. Where could the fault be?

The brothers talked about the problem that so perplexed them as they walked along the narrow ribbon of sand that separated the ocean from the inlets. They stopped to watch the flight of the gannets—great gulls with a wingspread of six feet—as they soared and dipped and soared again, finally landing on the beach just out of reach of the waves. Imitating the movements of the birds that flew with such ease, Will and Orv bent their elbows and wrists up and down as the wings were bent. But the answer was not there.

The weather was growing colder, and soon it would be too cold to live and work in the shed. Only a few tins of food remained to be cooked over the gasoline stove. Still, how could they leave until they had made successful flights in their new glider?

Finally, the answer came to Orville, one night, as he lay sleepless on his canvas bed.

He could hardly wait till morning to talk to Wilbur. When morning came, Orville told his brother about the idea he had had as he lay awake.

"I believe I have it, Will," Orv said, his voice shaking with excitement. "The tail shouldn't be stiff; it should move like a rudder. Then it would keep the glider level."

Wilbur listened with close attention. He was silent for a moment or two. Then he said, "You're right! And if we wire the rudder and the wings together, one lever can control both."

Soon after breakfast, they set to work on the new rudder.

In three days it was ready. During the next ten days, Will and Orv made seven hundred successful flights. The glider could now be balanced easily and guided up or down, as well as to the left or right.

Ten: December 17, 1903

The brothers were still not satisfied. They had mastered gliding, yes, but they longed to try a power machine. On the train back to Dayton from Kitty Hawk, they began to plan a flying machine that would have an engine and propellers.

Will wrote to a dozen factories describing the kind of engine they needed. It must be light, he said.

It must run at an even speed, and it must use little fuel. Did they make such an engine?

"An airplane engine? Never heard of such a thing! Some crank in Ohio thinks he's going to fly," the manufacturers laughed when they opened their mail. Into the wastebasket went most of Will's letters. A few firms replied, but they only expressed the same thoughts politely.

Will and Orv watched for the postman each day, hoping for word of an engine they could use. They had already started work on the new plane—they must find an engine somewhere.

While he waited for Will to sort through the mail one morning, Orv watched Charlie Taylor, their mechanic, as he worked on a bicycle. Charlie managed the shop now so the Wrights could have time for their experiments.

Taylor looked up from his work as Will shook his head in discouragement. Still there were no replies about an engine.

"If those fellows can't make an engine, why don't you try it yourselves?" he asked. "I'll help," the skilled mechanic added.

"Can you make an engine that will lift an airplane?" asked Orv.

"I believe I can," Charlie Taylor answered. And he did. Using a lathe and a drill press, the only metal-working machines the Wrights owned, with his own hands he built the first airplane engine in the back room of the bicycle shop.

Charlie Taylor was trained to follow blueprints. But there were no blueprints to follow. Will and Orv would talk about the engine. When they were sure what they wanted, one of them drew on a piece of scratch paper the engine part they had been discussing. Then Charlie Taylor nailed the sketch over his bench and went to work.

A little before Christmas, work began on the motor, and by the middle of February the shop was filled with fumes from the smoky, homemade engine. It was noisy and it smoked, but it worked!

One thing remained now, to make propeller blades to drive the plane through the air. If Wilbur and Orville had needed propellers for a boat, there would have been books with plans and charts to help them. But this was something new: propellers for the air. There was no one in the world who could help them.

Every line, every inch must be talked over in the shop, at the table, even after they were in bed. Katharine was so cheerful, so interested in what they were doing. But at last her nerves gave way and she exclaimed to her father, "If they don't stop arguing, I think I shall leave home!"

Bishop Wright laughed when he saw the shocked expression on the faces of his sons at Katharine's outburst. "Katharine is right, boys. You have argued a good deal lately. At times, it even sounded as if you were quarreling."

"But you don't think we are!" Orville countered. "Surely, you and Katharine know that we aren't even arguing! It's just—"

"It's just that Orv gives such good reasons for his opinions that he convinces me he is right," Wilbur calmly interjected. "By that time, he has switched and is standing up for what I said. So we don't seem to get anywhere."

Their father gave an understanding chuckle. He had noticed this trait, ever since they were little boys. Maybe that was why they seemed always to agree so perfectly in the end.

"Perhaps if you go off by yourselves and talk it over quietly, you can agree on a solution," he suggested with a twinkle in his kind eyes.

Will and Orv followed their father's suggestion, and the problem was quickly solved. They would make propellers based exactly on the measurements they had worked out in the wind tunnel. They would make two pairs of blades that should turn in opposite directions.

Now they were ready for Kitty Hawk.

Katharine gave a sigh of relief when her father said that he would be at home this year while Will and Orv were away. She did not like the idea of the engine! Of course, she had worried about her brothers each time they set off with their gliders. But they had always come back sun-tanned and well, as if they had really been on a vacation. And she could understand riding a great kite. But this was different. Now there would be not only the winds but also the power of the engine to control. "An engine in a kite?" she thought. This she could not understand. As soon as they left, she planned to go to the library and see what she could find. She really should know more about her brothers' hobby.

Bishop Wright and Katharine stood on the station platform with the two as they left for Kitty Hawk on September 23, 1903.

"Here, Son," Bishop Wright said, pressing a silver dollar in Wilbur's hand. "I believe you're still the banker."

"What's this for, Father?" Wilbur asked curiously.

"Keep it to send us a wire when you fly." Bishop Wright's voice rose confidently over the roar of the oncoming train.

They were headed to Kitty Hawk for the fourth time. As soon as they arrived, Wilbur and Orville started building a larger shed for the new plane. This was to be a larger plane with wings that would have a span of forty feet, six feet between the upper wing and the lower. Every part must be made strong to bear the weight of the 160-pound motor.

"I think we should test the engine on the ground before we put it in," Wilbur said the day the plane was assembled.

"Good idea," Orville agreed, starting the motor. And a good idea it was, for the hollow shafts of the propellers twisted out of shape with the first turn of the engine.

The brothers looked at each other helplessly. There was nothing to do but ask Charlie Taylor to send new shafts, and to wait in the cold, drafty camp until they came.

Postmaster Tate and some of the men from the Coast Guard station had heard about the new plane with an engine and came to see it. They went away feeling very sorry for the Wrights.

"Did you ever see worse luck?"

"What a pity they ever got the notion they could fly a machine like that!"

"Such fine fellows, too, to waste their time that way."

On November 28, the new shafts came, and the engine was started again—another setback! The new shafts cracked, and pieces of metal flew off as the propellers whirled.

"No matter if the shafts do weigh more, Will, they'll have to be solid steel." Orville's fingers were numb with cold as he removed the cracked shafts.

"How can we get solid shafts?" Wilbur watched his brother while he measured the propellers.

"Make them," said Orville.

"But where?" Wilbur looked out over the barren dunes.

"In the shop." Orville's shoulders drooped as he plodded over the sand to begin his journey to Dayton.

Wilbur stood looking after him as long as he could see him. "Why do we keep on, when everything goes against us?" he asked himself. He shivered in the wind and put his hands in his pockets. Absently, he fingered the coins there. Suddenly, he felt his father's silver dollar. That was the answer. They could not stop while their father and Katharine had faith in them.

When Orville went up the walk at 7 Hawthorne Street, Katharine rushed to the door. Frantically, she asked, "Where's Will? Has something happened to Will?"

Her father followed her into the hall, anxiously looking over her shoulder.

Quickly, Orville reassured them. "Will's all right. It's just those blamed propeller shafts. We're still having trouble."

Early the next morning, he was in the bicycle shop at work with Charlie Taylor on solid shafts. In a few days, he started on the weary journey back to Kitty Hawk, and reached there on December 11. The worst weather in years prevented trying out the machine for several days.

As Wilbur and Orville sat in their camp listening to the great waves pounding on the shore, a new worry was added to those about the engine and the plane.

"How long do you think this thing is going to keep up? It's less than two weeks until Christmas," Wilbur said, looking out of the small window in the end of the shed. He could see dark clouds moving like a procession across the windy skies.

"I know, and we've never in our lives missed a Christmas at home," Orville replied glumly. "I promised the children and Katharine we'd be back."

Lorin lived just three blocks from 7 Hawthorne Street, and his four children looked upon this house as a second home. Here their uncles played with them. Both Wilbur and Orville read to them, but Uncle Will was their favorite reader. His nieces and nephews demanded Gelett Burgess's *The Goops and How to Be Them* so often that Wilbur said he had probably read it through more times than any other book in the world. When Wilbur tired of reading, their Uncle Orv entertained them with games or took them to the kitchen to make candy.

While Wilbur and Orville scanned the heavens in discouragement, Katharine, so many miles away, also felt under a cloud of depression. When she visited the public library to read about her brothers' hobby, she found nothing to encourage her. There were magazine articles by Professor Newcomb and other college professors who proved positively in the most scientific terms that man would never fly. There were accounts of attempts at flight, all ending in failure. The most recent was one just made by Professor Langley of the Smithsonian, whose books Will and Orv had read with such interest when they first took up gliding.

She hesitated to speak to her father about these things she had read. It might seem that she lacked faith in her brothers, that she was not loyal to them. But she wondered.

"Why do the boys think they will be able to fly when everyone says it is impossible?"

"Not everyone, Katharine." Bishop Wright smiled into her troubled face. "Not everyone. The dream of flight has always been in the hearts of a few."

Her father was a scholarly man. And drawing upon his scholar's knowledge of the past, he told his daughter about some of the dreamers. He spoke of Roger Bacon, who in 1250 wrote, "it is possible to make engines for flying" and "wings to beat the aire." He spoke, too, of Leonardo da Vinci's notebooks made four hundred years before, with their sketches of helicopters and parachutes; and of his prophecy that "Man shall fly like a mighty swan."

"This same dream seems to be in the hearts of your brothers. Who can tell? They may be the ones to make it come true, at last." Bishop Wright paused, and then added reverently, as if he had been in his pulpit, "God willing, I believe they will fly."

As he finished, his eyes were glowing—glowing with the same light that shone in them as he set out to meet unknown dangers in Oregon more than forty years before. He had not been afraid to be a pioneer. He was glad his sons were not afraid.

Katharine was radiant, her hope restored. "I believe so, too," she said proudly. She had no doubt now that her brothers belonged in the company of Bacon and da Vinci, not of Professor Newcomb.

The skies over Kitty Hawk finally cleared. On December 14, Wilbur and Orville wheeled out their machine. They had tossed a coin to see which should ride first. Wilbur won, but his ride was short. The plane lifted from the sand for only three seconds. Because it landed at a point lower than the place from which it started, the Wrights were too conscientious to call it a flight. And, in landing, the plane was damaged. It would take at least two days to make repairs, a delay that would bring Christmas nearer, without a successful flight.

When Wilbur and Orville wakened on the morning of December 17, they were grimly determined to succeed. There was a strong wind from the north, and puddles of water around the camp were covered with ice. But the day was fair, in spite of the wind. They decided to make their first real attempt at flight with power. The Wrights had promised to signal the Coast Guard station when they were ready for a flight, so Orville put up a white flag on the shed. Soon three guards arrived from the station, along with a man and a boy who lived in the settlement.

It was Orville's turn to have the first ride. At 10:35 he climbed in the plane. He started the engine, which was fastened on the lower wing. He let it run a few minutes to warm up. It shook the whole plane. Orville hoped it would not shake itself loose. Wilbur stood beside the plane, his face tense and anxious.

"Ready?" he shouted above the clatter and roar of the engine.

His brother waved and released the wire that held the rudder.

Wilbur ran beside the machine, holding the wing to balance it. The men from the Coast Guard station held their breath and then let out a mighty shout as the plane darted up and sailed along, ten feet above the ground. The flight ended 120 feet from where it began, and Orville was in the air just twelve seconds.

It was a flight of only twelve seconds! But those few seconds seemed longer than the many months of uncertainty and work that had made possible this

free and unfettered fragment of time. Never before in the history of the world had a machine carrying a man lifted itself into the air by its own power.

The plane settled gently on the sand. Orville climbed out. Silently, he and Wilbur shook hands, too filled with emotion to talk at this unbelievable moment. Then they clasped hands and jumped up and down on the sand like boys, while the men who had witnessed the flight crowded around excitedly.

Now they could honestly say the things they had been thinking for three years.

"We used to watch you from the windows of the station, standing on the beach for hours, just looking at the gulls. We felt sorry for you. Now you're flying, too."

How Wilbur and Orville laughed! They could laugh now. They had not laughed for days.

"We knew you thought we were just a pair of nuts," Orville teased their visitors.

"There were times when I thought so, myself." A tone of seriousness was in Wilbur's voice.

"There's just one thing I'd like to know now," said a coast guard, as he pushed toward the center of the group. "How long have you two been working at this flying business?"

The brothers looked at each other. How long, indeed? They remembered the jerky flight of the bamboo and paper helicopter that their father had brought them so many years ago when they were children.

"All of our lives," Wilbur answered quietly.

Now it was his turn to try the plane, while Orville ran into the shed to get warm over the driftwood fire they had made in a large tin can. There were white caps on the Atlantic, and a wintry wind blew from the shore. No one had thought of warm clothes for flying because no one had flown before.

Once more, Orville was in the plane. This time he went twice as far.

Wilbur made the last flight of the day, exactly at noon. The plane was under better control now, and took off into the wind like a great bird. One hundred, two hundred, three hundred, on it flew and did not land until it was eight hundred and fifty-two feet from its starting point. It had been in the air fifty-nine seconds!

Orville knew what Wilbur meant when he said, "I guess it's time to use Father's dollar, Orv." He pulled it from his pocket. It had been there all the time he was flying!

It was past noon, and they had had quite a morning. They were hungry. So Orville prepared lunch as usual; and as usual, Wilbur washed the dishes. Then they walked four miles along the storm-swept beach to send a telegram to Dayton.

"Be sure to tell them we'll be home for Christmas," Wilbur said eagerly as Orville wrote out the message.

Eleven: HOME FOR CHRISTMAS

By the time the Western Union messenger boy reached 7 Hawthorne Street, it was late afternoon, almost time for Katharine to come home from school.

Slowly, Bishop Wright took the telegram that was addressed to him. The message must be from Will and Orv.

> Success four flights thursday morning all against twenty one mile wind started from level with engine power alone average speed through air thirty one miles longest 57 seconds inform press home christmas. Orevelle Wright[1]

---

[1] This first telegraph home had two transcription errors. It should have read 59 seconds, and Orville's name was spelled "Orevelle."

The news was good—so good that he could scarcely believe it. Then Katharine came, and they read together the news of man's first flight—read the news in this room where so much of it began, with the twisted corners of a pasteboard box, with a dream kept in the hearts of her brothers and a purpose locked in the stronghold of their minds.

Such wonderful news must be shared. Lorin must hear it; Charlie Taylor must be told. Katharine sent a telegram to Octave Chanute telling him that "the boys" had made four flights.

"Inform Press," the message from his sons had said, so this Bishop Wright proudly tried to do. He could imagine the headlines in the morning paper! "Dayton Boys are First to Fly" or "Dayton Boys Pioneers in Flying."

He asked Lorin to take the telegram to the Associated Press.

But the Associated Press representative in the office of the Dayton Journal said the telegram had no news value. It was plain he did not believe a word about the flight. The scoop of the century lay on his desk, and he yawned! When subscribers to the Journal opened their papers the next morning, they saw the headline he had written. "Stores are Filled With Christmas Shoppers." This was news!

A young reporter in Norfolk, Virginia, the only city of any size near Kitty Hawk, heard about the telegram which Wilbur and Orville sent. Since he had not seen the flight, the plane, or the Wrights, he made up a story about them and about what he thought might have taken place. Nothing about the story was true except the fact that the Wrights had flown. He tried to sell it to more than twenty newspapers, but only a few would buy.

Editors all over the country had read the articles that so distressed Katharine. If famous men of science had proved it was impossible to fly, why should they be expected to believe that two unknown bicycle mechanics had done it?

The papers that did print the story sent out from Norfolk said only "it is reported." The editors seemed to be saying, "Here is a fairy tale. We are too clever to believe it. Do you think men can really fly?"

Wilbur and Orville arrived in Dayton two days before Christmas. Katharine and their father met them at the station. The trolley car was crowded with Christmas shoppers,

loaded down with parcels. Will and Orv had not expected to be met with a brass band, but they did think it was strange that no one mentioned their flight. And did they imagine it? When they tried to speak, some of their neighbors who were in the car looked away.

Katharine saw this, and leaned forward nervously to speak to her brothers. "Everyone seems to have been Christmas shopping."

"We've done ours," said Orville, winking at Wilbur. They were bringing Katharine a set of beautiful pearl-handled knives, for which she had often wished.

"Yes, and this time you're not getting your present before Christmas," said Wilbur.

Bishop Wright joined in their laughter as they all remembered Sterchens's doll.

"Here's our stop," said Wilbur, looking out the window in the dusk. He reached for the bell cord.

Wilbur and Orville looked around contentedly when they went in the house. The living room was fragrant and merry with Christmas greens. How pleasant it seemed after all their weeks in the bare camp at Kitty Hawk! They went to the table in the center of the room and began looking through the papers and magazines there.

"I hope you saved the newspapers for us," Orville said eagerly. "I can't wait to see what the Journal had to say about our flight."

Katharine and her father looked at each other, but neither one had the heart to speak.

"You took them our wire?" Orville continued.

"Yes," Bishop Wright answered in a dull voice. "Yes, they had your wire."

Something was wrong! The brothers looked searchingly at their father and Katharine.

She could not restrain her indignation any longer. "There weren't any papers to save. They didn't even print your telegram."

"But why?" Wilbur asked, puzzled. "We were sure they would think it was news when we flew for 59 seconds."

"59 seconds? The wire said 57," his father exclaimed in surprise.

"That was a mistake," said Will.

"What difference does it make?" Orville broke in fiercely. "They didn't believe we flew at all. Wasn't that it?"

"Yes, Orv, nobody in Dayton believes you flew." Katharine could not keep her lips from trembling. Will and Orv had been so happy. Now they were stunned by what she told them. She could not bear to see their homecoming spoiled. She had planned so long for this evening.

Wilbur saw how deep was her disappointment. Putting his arm around her, he said affectionately, "It really doesn't matter. It's just so good to be at home that it doesn't matter at all."

But Orville felt in his pocket to be sure the roll of film was still there.

"Just wait until they see my pictures. Then they'll have to believe." He had set up his camera on the morning of December 17, and one of the coast guards snapped the plane while it was in the air.

"I mean to keep a record of our flights," he added.

Katharine had planned her brothers' favorite dinner. While she bustled around the kitchen cooking a steak, with baked potatoes and winter vegetables brought up from the cellar, she wondered if the potatoes would remind them, as they did her, of their picnics in the woods. Their first "invention" had worked. How she hoped this one would work, too!

She could hear the excited voices of Wilbur and Orville as they sat in the living room answering their father's questions and telling him about the flights on December 17. This did not sound to her like talk about a hobby. It sounded like the talk of men who had found their lifework. She did not yet understand how a man could travel through the air in a machine. But she believed that her brothers had done it.

Now, indeed, the hobby was to become a lifework. They could scarcely wait to begin a new plane. Charlie Taylor would run the shop. Wilbur was thirty-six; Orville was thirty-two. They had been first printers, then bicycle mechanics. Now they had made their last bicycle.

Twelve: Some Astonished Cows

Orville was twisting the last screw in the framework. He straightened up and stood back to look
over the new plane.

"It's a beauty, Will, just a beauty. Look at it now!"
he exclaimed.

His brother walked around the plane, its steel
wires gleaming in the spring sunshine. Its wings were
white and untouched by weather.

"It sure looks good to me, Orv," he said after his inspection. "It looks fine. But how are we going to find out if it will fly?"

This question had been in their minds for weeks. The time had come to settle it. They had made some changes in the design of this plane. It was heavier than the one they flew at Kitty Hawk. How Will and Orv longed for the open, sandy beaches of Kitty Hawk! But Kitty Hawk was too far away.

"Let's take a ride on the trolley this afternoon, out toward Simm's Station," Orville suggested. "We might see a piece of land that we could rent."

Near Simm's station, eight miles from Dayton, they saw a fairly level cow pasture. It belonged to Torrence Huffman, president of a bank in Dayton. When the Wrights asked if they might rent his pasture, he said, "I won't rent it to you. I won't charge you a cent, boys. You're welcome to use it. All I ask is: don't run over my cows. Just drive them out of the way."

It was not much of a flying field, not as they are known today. There were holes and piles of dirt; there were trees and bushes. Danger was added by the electric wires, which supplied power for the trolley line running beside the pasture.

Mr. Huffman's astonished cows were there, also. They had to be driven out of the way each time the flying machine was pulled from a shed in one corner of the field. If even one of these cows could return, they would be more than astonished. For their pasture is now in the center of a modern airfield, with planes taking off and landing constantly, day and night!

Every day in the spring and summer of the years 1904 and 1905, when it did not rain and the wind was right, either Wilbur or Orville made flights of increasing length, circling the pasture again and again in their new plane.

In a letter to scientists in Great Britain, Wilbur wrote, "The machine passed through all of these flights without the slightest damage. In each of these flights we returned frequently to the starting point, passing high over the heads of the spectators."

Strange as it seems now, the spectators of whom Wilbur wrote had been few. When the new plane was ready for its trial flight in May 1904, Will and Orv invited the Dayton and Cincinnati newspapers to send reporters. Ten or twelve came, but most came unwillingly. They were smart. You could not fool them. The Wrights would not fly. Nobody in the world could fly.

It was a dreadful day for the Wright brothers. In the morning there was too much wind for them to start the plane safely. Then there was no wind at all. Hours passed. Will and Orv still waited for the right wind.

The reporters became more and more angry. They glared at the plane, so new and shining; they glared at Will and Orv so calmly waiting beside it.

They had not wanted to come in the first place, they told each other. Did the Wrights think they had nothing better to do than to stand around all day in a cow pasture looking at a big kite sitting on the ground?

In disgust, they left the field. Not one of them came back.

There were some good flying days, however. Then the motorman of the trolley would slow down as it passed the field so that his passengers could stick their heads out of the windows to see the plane.

Bishop Wright went to the field whenever he was at home and timed his sons' flights with his big pocket watch.

Katharine would have been proud to have some of the other teachers in her school go with her to see Wilbur and Orville fly. But no one was interested. Like the newspaper reporters, they did not really believe the Wrights could fly.

One man in Dayton said, "The Wright boys are neglecting their business and wasting time on that silly flying machine."

Others remarked, "Those lazy boys don't want work. They'd rather let their sister and their father support them. What a cross the bishop has to bear!"

Katharine was filled with intense indignation. How could people say such dreadful and untrue things about her brothers? She longed to rush out to defend them. They had never used any money but their own—money they had worked day and night in the bicycle shop to earn. It was their own money that had built the plane, money they had saved in the Building and Loan Association.

But what could she do? Everywhere she went it was the same—in the grocery store, in the butcher shop, as she passed along the street. Sometimes it was only a word—"crazy" or "lazy" or "kites." Sometimes it was a joke told with a sly wink. "Dayton can't laugh at Detroit any more about Ford and his horseless carriage. We have the Wrights and their flying machine."

No matter what was said, or where, it was like a knife turning in Katharine's heart. She loved her brothers so much, even more, she thought, since people made fun of them for flying.

So Katharine took the long trolley ride to the field alone. She worried all of the time for fear the plane would crash and Will and Orv be killed.

Whenever the plane landed suddenly, Mrs. Beard, who lived in the farmhouse nearby, ran out with her arnica bottle, just in case it might be needed for cuts and scratches. But for Katharine there was no such relief in action. She stood, unable to move, until the one who had piloted the machine climbed out.

Over and over she asked herself, "How can they expect the air to hold them up?"

One evening, when the three had come back from the field together, Katharine asked her brothers this very question and added, "How can you just sit up there on nothing?"

Orville threw up his hands in dismay. For years he and Wilbur had studied the air. How could he explain at the supper table things it had taken them so long to learn?

But Wilbur was more patient—he enjoyed explaining things. He had planned to be a teacher before his accident on the ice.

"We aren't just sitting up there on nothing, as you call it, Katharine. Because you can't see it or take it in your hand doesn't mean that air isn't real. Why, it's as real—" he looked about the table and touched the goblet near his plate, "it's as real as water or as milk, if we could only see it. "You know what force it has, when it isn't just air, but gathers itself into wind."

Katharine said, "But, Will, you still haven't answered my question. How can you expect the air to hold you up? And even though it does hold you up, what makes the plane move through it?"

Wilbur thought a minute. How to answer this really stumped him! Then he held out his hands, one above the other. "It's just like your fan, Katharine, when you try to cool yourself off," he said slowly. "As you move the fan you feel the force of the air against it; the bigger the fan, the more the force, and the faster you move the fan, the more the force."

Wilbur showed what he meant by using his hands. "My hand on the bottom is the air pushing against the wings. At the same time, the air going over the top of the plane speeds up as it passes over and pulls just as my top hand would pull. It is as if I held the plane in my hands. The air that goes past the bottom of the plane pushes up, and the air that goes past the top pulls up. We call this 'lift,' and there we sit, safe as anything, held up by the air.

"Now, Orv, let's borrow your hands." Wilbur pulled his brother's hands toward him, putting one hand in front and one hand behind his own. "See, the hand in front is a propeller. As it rotates, it pushes the air back over the plane and pulls it forward. Orv's other hand is the air pulling back. We call this 'drag' for it is what keeps the plane from going too fast. Do you remember the pasteboard box?"

Katharine nodded, smiling.

Wilbur smiled, too, as he recalled that night. "I suppose Orv and I looked pretty silly, so happy because we had found we could twist a box. But that was how we learned to bend the frame of our glider, to make a new shape for the wind to hit, the way a gull steadies itself with its wings."

Katharine stood amazed as she looked at her brothers. In the space between their hands, Will's above and below, Orv's to the left and right, she seemed to see a plane. She knew Will had tried to answer her questions simply, because he had watched her struggles with mathematics from her multiplication-table days on. But this she could understand and remember. Their plane was in her brothers' hands.

Thirteen: RETURN TO KITTY HAWK

I f the people of Dayton did not think the eight-mile
trolley ride to the Huffman pasture was a journey
worth taking, there were others who thought that
four thousand miles was not too far to come to see
the invention of the Wright brothers. Agents for the
French government came all the way from Paris to
talk about buying a plane. The British government
sent agents from London.

But for all who came, Wilbur and Orville had only one answer, "The United States has the first right to our invention."

Great was their shock, then, at the reply they received when they offered to the War Department in Washington all of their knowledge of flying and the results of their discoveries. Far from appreciating the Wrights' patriotism, the officials sent only a form letter stating that no money could be given for experiments in flight.

Will and Orv had not asked for money. They had sent proof that their machine had already flown. It was discouraging to receive a reply that had very little relation to what they had written.

But they were so sure that their plane would be of great help to their country for scouting and delivering messages in time of war, that they swallowed their pride and wrote once more. This time they explained that they did not wish to sell their machine to a European government unless they were compelled to do so.

Still the War Department refused to believe that there was a machine that would fly. Their answer to this letter was word for word like the first. The Washington officials did not openly scoff. They did worse. They ignored the whole thing. It was simply too wild, too fantastic for official notice.

Will and Orv had come almost to the end of their savings. Money, not big money, but enough to get by, became important.

But the thing that turned their hearts to lead was the future of their dream. It would take government backing to bring that to completion. In the entire world, the Wrights alone held the secret of flight. Had all their work been for nothing? Could it be that after solving a riddle that had teased great minds through the ages, their discovery would be rejected?

Somewhere there must be men of vision. The French had sought the rights to the airplane as an answer to the new guns the Germans were making in the great Krupp works. And so it was to France that Wilbur sailed on the Campania. In the hold was the crated plane that he hoped to sell there.

In a short time, Orville joined his brother in Paris. At first, they stayed at the Meurice, a beautiful hotel on the Rue de Rivoli. Formal attire was required at meetings with government officials so the Wrights bought dress suits and silk hats and wore them for the first time in their lives.

But they waited week after week for members of the French Cabinet to agree on terms. Their money began to dwindle. They moved to a cheaper hotel and amused themselves in inexpensive ways, visiting art galleries and museums at a cost of only a few francs. On sunny days they helped the little boys and girls who played in the Tuileries Gardens sail their toy boats in the shallow pools around the fountains. The French children soon learned to know them and watched for them every afternoon. Escaping from their nurses, they ran down the path to meet them.

"The Americans, the Americans, our friends," they called.

"The children are the only ones in France who remember we exist," Wilbur said bitterly one afternoon as he and Orville sat on a bench near the fountains.

Suddenly, Orville stood up. He had reached a decision if the French officials had not. "We've waited long enough. It's time we moved on. We'll go to Berlin."

The Wrights were received with great honor in Berlin, but the Kaiser and his Cabinet did not feel they needed anything more than their own Zeppelin balloons, of which they were so proud. Two more discouraged Americans it would be hard to imagine as Will and Orv returned to Dayton without selling their machine.

But while they were in Europe, the United States government had decided that there might be such a thing as a flying machine, after all. The War Department offered a prize for a machine carrying two men, which would fly at the rate of forty miles an hour and stay in the air for an hour.

Forty-one people wrote to ask about the contest, but there were only three legal bids. One of these was quickly withdrawn. The second man went to Dayton and asked the Wrights to make a plane for him! When they refused, he also withdrew from the contest, and their bid was accepted on February 8, 1908.

Angry articles appeared in magazines and newspapers. Editors blamed the War Department for this foolish waste of the taxpayers' money. They said that if there really were a machine that would fly it would be the most important invention in the history of the world. Its inventor could claim millions rather than $25,000 as its price.

But President Theodore Roosevelt had heard about the Wrights. He believed in them and told the secretary of war, William Howard Taft, to go ahead with the contract.

Early in 1908, about the time the United States' offer was made, a French company sent word they wished to buy the patents for France. Their terms also included a flight of an hour in a plane carrying two men. But in addition, three pupils must be taught to fly.

After more than four years of waiting, at last the Wrights were to have a chance to prove their plane, Orville in his own country and Wilbur in France.

How excited Katharine was at this double good fortune! It was hard for her to keep her mind on Latin. Now she could buy steak for her brothers as often as she wished. Now her father could have some new books. For herself she wished nothing. She could not think of a thing she wanted, only that people would believe Will and Orv really could fly.

The contracts that brought such happiness to Katharine brought also a problem to vex her brothers. As before, they sought the solution in the old shed, the wide sand and sea, the steady winds of Kitty Hawk. All of the flying Wilbur and Orville had done was with the pilot riding flat, just as they had coasted on their sleds when they were boys. Although it was very tiring on the back of the neck for the pilot to keep raising his head to watch for obstructions, this had been good enough for short flights, with one man in the plane. But both the American and French contracts required that the plane carry a passenger as well as a pilot. So new controls must be worked out for steering the machine from a sitting position.

When the brothers reached Kitty Hawk, they found the sidewalls and rafters of their camp still standing, but the winter storms had ripped the sheeting from the roof and blown down the north door. The new shed was in ruins.

With the help of two carpenters, Will and Orv repaired the old building to house their plane and built new and larger living quarters.

Deep sand had drifted from the dunes, but when it was cleared away, the camp looked almost as it had when they had closed it and hurried home for Christmas on that December day which seemed so much more than four and a half years ago.

Poking around in the corner of the shed, which served as a kitchen when he and Will had lived there before, Orv found his biscuit tins, packed away in a box under the old stove. They were rusty.

"I can scour them up, and they will be good enough to use again," he said as he pulled them out.

Will laughed. "That's good. It wouldn't seem like Kitty Hawk without your biscuits."

Some of the coast guards who had seen the Wrights' first glider tried out on the dunes in 1900 were still stationed at Kitty Hawk. As soon as they heard that Will and Orv had returned, they hurried to the camp.

"We just reckoned you'd be back when we read about the contracts," said one heartily, as he pounded Orville's back with the affectionate familiarity of an old friend.

"Sure, where else would they go when there's something big to do?" a second guard asked proudly. "What are you fellows up to now?" he added.

These men had a right to know. Had they not shared days on the dunes, watching each year as the spread of the gliders grew like the wings of fledgling birds? In the end, they would share the miracle of that stormy December morning when they saw "man fly like a mighty swan."

So Wilbur and Orville explained quite simply the changes necessary in their plane. They said they would have to practice using the new controls before they could be sure of success in the test flights for the United States government and France.

The Wrights would have been glad to talk about their plans also to the newspapermen whose presence in Kitty Hawk was reported to them by the amused coast guards. The reporters chose to keep out of sight, hiding in the scrub pines and watching Wilbur and Orville through field glasses. Men from important papers in New York and London crowded into one small boarding house at night. Each morning, they set out at dawn with food and water so they would not have to move from their hiding place. Sun or rain, sand fleas or mosquitoes could not drive them out for fear the fliers would see them.

The achievements of the Wrights had been so long ignored by the press that no reporter could believe that they would fly and reveal the secrets of their new plane if they knew they were being watched.

But the Wrights did fly. And on May 14, the astounded reporters saw a sight that made them forget to hide, forget their discomforts, forget even to click their cameras. Incredible, impossible—but they were seeing what no one had ever seen before—two men sitting in a plane as it flew over the beach.

The plane was new, and there were new ways in the air. But in the camp the ways were old. It was

easy for Will and Orv to take up once more the pattern of living they had followed in those other days at Kitty Hawk. So much had happened that those days seemed far away until they returned to the familiar sandy reaches of Kill Devil Hill.

Now they remembered everything about those days. As they sat by the fire in the evenings after flights in the new plane, they talked of all the ways in which they had tried to make flight possible. But the thing they remembered best of all—the one thing neither of them could ever forget—they did not talk about. They just looked in the fire and thought about it—the way they felt on December 17, 1903, when they knew that men could fly. That was not a thing to be talked about, at least by two who were known as the "Silent Wrights."

Fourteen: New Skies

A slender man wearing a plain business suit and a woolen cap alighted from the trolley near Fort Myer, Virginia. Unnoticed, he walked to a corner of the parade ground and stood beside the flying machine that rested there. No reporter rushed to interview him. A thousand people crowded around the sides of the parade ground, pushing and shoving to get a good look at the plane. But no one recognized Orville Wright, the inventor.

In a skeptical group nearby stood the high-ranking officers who had been ordered to witness the tests of the Wright plane. How bored they were! These men had spent their lives learning the science of war: the massing of men on foot, thundering cavalry charges, the firing of great cannons. How could they believe that in this frail and untried contraption—a few wood ribs from an ash tree, some steel wires, muslin wings, and a small engine—there was a power that should control the fate of nations?

An eager light shone in the eyes of the young officers who watched from the edge of the crowd while Orville's skillful fingers tested the controls of his plane. But even they, with all the dreams of youth, could not imagine on this September 3, 1908, how such a machine would change war making before they should wear on their own shoulders the emblems of rank now worn by their senior officers.

A few more turns of the controls and Orville was ready. Katharine and Father Wright in Dayton, Wilbur in France, were waiting. They had all waited so long for this day, waited too long, already. "May as well start," Orv said to himself. "Start to fly for the government of the United States of America!"

The crowd milled about, looking curiously at the plane. One moment it was there on the ground. The next it was in the air! Without warning, it rose and began circling the parade ground. The amazed spectators gave such a gasp of astonishment that it seemed to come from one great throat.

Now the reporters rushed to interview Orville. Now they knew who he was!

For several days the test flights continued, and there was no question that the plane had more than met the conditions of the contract when Orville flew for an hour and fifteen minutes on September 12.

The most eager in the group of young officers who watched the flights was Lieutenant Thomas Selfridge, a graduate of West Point. When Orville made his final flight on September 17, Lieutenant Selfridge asked to go along as passenger. This flight ended in t r a g e d y,

the only accident of Orville Wright's career. A rudder wire broke, and the plane crashed. Orville was severely injured and always limped slightly as a result. Lieutenant Selfridge lost his life. This daring young officer was killed instantly; he was the first army officer to die in a plane.

On regaining consciousness, Orville's concern was not for himself, but for Katharine. He knew how alarmed she would be to hear about the crash.

"Tell my sister not to worry," he said in a weak voice.

But Katharine did worry. How could she help it? She did not wait for more news. As soon as she learned of the accident, she closed the door of her schoolroom for the last time. Her brother needed her. Nothing else mattered. She must go to him.

At Le Mans, France, thousands of miles away, Wilbur got the news. He longed to cancel his test flights for the French contract and rush to his brother's side. How could he fly when Orv might not even live? But he could not leave. He had never felt so alone. Now he would have to carry their dreams by himself.

A cable from Katharine soon brought wonderful news. Orville would recover! Wilbur could prepare for the trial flights with a light heart.

His flight was better and smoother than Orville's. On September 21, just four days after his brother's accident, Wilbur finished his test flight in France by making a record of more than an hour and a half in the air.

For this important occasion, he dressed as he always did, except when he was working on the plane in overalls. He wore an ordinary gray suit and cap and a white shirt with a high, starched collar. No one had yet thought of a pilot's helmet and warm aviator's jacket.

When he completed his record-making flight, Wilbur's only thought was of Katharine and Orville. He could imagine Orville lying in his bed, wrapped in bandages, watching the clock, figuring the difference in time—waiting. Katharine would be sitting near, making a brave attempt to amuse him by reading aloud, trying not to look at the clock.

Wilbur did not stop to listen to the shouts of the crowds that had witnessed his flight. He did not even wait to be kissed on both cheeks by the many enthusiastic Frenchmen who swarmed over the field. He ducked out and, still shivering from the chill of such a long time in the open plane, he hurried to the cable office. As he wrote out the cable he said, "This will cheer Orville up a bit." He had no thought of pride over his astonishing flight. He was happy because the news would bring joy to his family.

The flight was made from a field near Le Mans, a village 125 miles from Paris. It had been difficult to find what Wilbur called a "good pasture" near the great city. When he was told that there was level country around Le Mans, he went there by train. At first, the only open space he could find was a rather small racetrack. So he was very happy when he was given permission to fly from a large field that was used by the French army as a testing ground for new cannons. A shelter was quickly put up for the plane. Wilbur could not understand why the French always spoke of this rough building as a "hangar." He never called it anything but his "shed."

Wilbur lived in the shed, sleeping on a canvas cot near the plane. He continued to do so, although he was soon the hero of France. The French know how to treat a hero! Wilbur was showered with invitations. Even the cab drivers of Le Mans asked to be allowed to give a dinner in his honor! His presence in Le Mans with his plane had brought them so much business that they were overcome with gratitude.

Regular excursion parties were organized to bring people from distant parts of France, and several trains brought visitors each day from Paris. The visitors who understood a little English translated Wilbur's most casual remarks into flowery French for the benefit of eager admirers.

Postcard pictures of the "American Aviator" were sold in the streets everywhere in France; from the great boulevards of Paris to the narrow, cobbled streets of remote mountain villages.

After much urging, Wilbur finally consented to attend a few functions given in his honor by clubs interested in flying, but always on condition that he would not be asked to make a speech. At a dinner given in Paris by the Aero Club, however, the presiding officer was so thrilled to have the idol of France present that he broke his promise and called upon him.

Wilbur excused himself by a reply that was quoted with delight by all the wits of Paris.

"I know of only one bird, the parrot, that talks," he said, "and it can't fly very high."

On the last day of the year, Wilbur made one more flight from Le Mans. He made a new record, staying in the air two hours and twenty minutes. For this astonishing feat he was given an award of 20,000 francs, or $4,000, by the Michelin Company.

To complete the French contract, three pilots must be taught to fly. Winter had come in earnest to Le Mans, and it was too stormy to train them there. Pau, a lovely resort town near the Pyrenees Mountains, had been agreed upon as a suitable place.

As he packed the plane for shipment to the south of France, Wilbur hummed and whistled all the lively tunes he and Orville had sung when they were boys working together on their "inventions." This year of 1908, which had begun in discouragement and unbelief, had ended happily for the Wrights. Orville's flights in the United States and his own in France had at last convinced the world that flying was not only possible but practical. Orville was recovering from his accident. In a few days, he and Katharine would sail to join Wilbur in Paris.

Fifteen: Wings for the World

There were no "Silent Wrights" the night the three met in Paris. There was so much to tell, so much to hear, since they had parted.

Wilbur must catch up on the news at home; he had not been in Dayton for ten months. Figures about record-breaking flights could wait.

"How is Father?" he inquired eagerly.

"Wonderful as ever," Orville answered.

"He sent you his love," Katharine added.

"How did you celebrate his birthday? I hated to miss that almost as much as Christmas."

"I planned to invite some of his friends and have a real birthday party, but he said all he wanted was a good home dinner," Katharine replied. "We put the cable you sent him on the table at your place, Will," she smiled at her brother. "I baked a cake from the 'Birthday Cake Recipe' Mother used when we were children. It turned out real well."

"I'll say it did!" Orville exclaimed. "Katharine decorated it, too. Father said he could never blow out eighty-two candles, so she put the dates in the middle, instead."

1826–1908

What changes lay between those dates written in pink frosting on a birthday cake! Every change was written indelibly on the pages of history!

When Milton Wright was born, his country was twenty-four states, with thousands of unexplored miles stretching across the continent. These eighty-two years of his life had seen America grow into a great country, united and strong at home, a world power abroad. These years had seen sailing ships and pony express; they had seen transcontinental trains and the submarine. But the greatest wonder of all had come from Milton Wright's own home.

"You should see him," Orville continued. "He's the first one up in the morning, reading the paper before breakfast to see if he can find anything about the Wright family."

"Oh!" exclaimed Wilbur. "Don't tell me the *Dayton Journal* now believes in flight!"

"Not only believes, but believes on the front page," Katharine said proudly. "Whenever Father finds something about either of you boys he cuts it out. Then he bounces downtown to show the clippings to his friends."

Bishop Wright's hair and his square-cut beard were white now, not black as when he brought the toy helicopter to his boys, Will and Orv. But he still wore a long-tailed minister's coat and moved down the street almost as vigorously as he did on that faraway afternoon.

No longer did people avoid him on the streets of Dayton. They were proud now to stop to shake the hand of the father of two such famous men. In fact, they went out of their way to show that they knew the Wright brothers. They had called them "weird" for many years—but not this year. This year, the most talked-about men in the world were the Wrights.

Sometimes there was a twinkle in their father's eyes as he listened to this praise of Will and Orv. He wondered that the neighbors could so soon forget how they had laughed at "the Wright boys and their kites." But it did not matter now. It was his sons, not theirs, who would soon go to Germany as guests of the Kaiser. It was his sons who would go to Rome in a few months upon the invitation of the king, there to see their plane drawn through the streets by horses from the royal stables, through the streets of the Caesars—along the Appian Way where Saint Paul walked to his martyrdom.

The hotel in Paris where the Wrights were reunited had buzzed with excitement when Wilbur's letter came, asking that rooms be reserved. The manager felt so highly honored to be host to the famous aviators that he provided a suite with a sitting room and insisted that they have supper there.

As Katharine watched the two smiling waiters deftly cover a small table with snowy linen and set it with thin china and gleaming silver bearing the monogram of the famous hotel, she tingled with delight. This was just as she had dreamed it would be! And what was more, Will had said she was to have her breakfast in bed! She could remember only a few times when she had been so ill that Will or Orv had brought a tray to her room. Never in her life had she breakfasted in bed!

There was something she had meant to ask Will. As soon as the supper table was wheeled away and the Wrights were alone once more she said, "Now. I want to see those medals you wrote were the size of a small can."

Wilbur laughed and went into his bedroom. He came back carrying the cardboard box in which he kept the trophies he had won since coming to France.

Opening the box, he dumped the medals in his sister's lap.

"There now, see what you think."

It was true. Some of them were indeed the size of a small can. Carefully, Katharine lifted them, reading the inscription on each shining disk. As she turned them over in her fingers and arranged them in a row on the wide window ledge, Will and Orv began to talk about the things each had discovered while making his trial flights. They could improve the next plane they built. Each time they built a plane it must be better.

Katharine pulled aside the heavy damask curtains and sat looking out at the lights of the city that shone so brightly in the crisp air of winter. Across the avenue, beyond the gardens, she recognized the dim outlines of the Louvre. Tomorrow she would go there. She would walk on the marble floors where great kings and queens once walked. At last, she would see the treasures of this most famous palace. The Venus de Milo, the Winged Victory, Leonardo da Vinci's Mona Lisa. Three hundred years before, she remembered, an emperor had looked from the windows of this palace and declared, "Other cities are merely cities; Paris is a world."

A world to an emperor! What would it be to a schoolteacher? Tomorrow she, Katharine Wright, from Dayton, Ohio, would explore this world.

On and on her brothers talked of "wind lift" and "rudder stress," but Katharine would not leave them, although she began to nod sleepily. It was too wonderful to know she was really in Paris and that she and Will and Orv were together.

But when tomorrow came, it was not as a school-teacher from Dayton that Katharine explored the world of Paris. It was as Mlle. (mademoiselle) Wright, sister of the world-famous aviators, the Messrs. Wright. As soon as the three stepped into the Rue de Rivoli, expecting to window-shop their way down this fascinating street, people seemed to come from every direction and follow them like a procession.

Young dressmakers' assistants in their skimpy black frocks forgot their errands and used the big boxes they carried to make a way for themselves into the center of the crowd. Apprentice boys in coarse smocks and knitted berets pushed in to gape at the Americans. Shoppers, both men and women, were drawn into the stream of enthusiastic, gesticulating admirers.

And why not? Had not each of them bought a picture of Wilbur Wright, and was it not now hanging near the clock at home? But yes!

Will and Orv looked at each other. As usual, they were thinking of the same thing—those days, two years ago, when, unnoticed by anyone, they had walked this street, uncertain, discouraged, waiting for the French government to accept or reject their plane. As their funds dwindled with the waiting, how often they had looked at the glittering displays in these windows hoping to find something not too expensive for them to take home to Katharine.

When the three Wrights entered a shop, the crowd waited outside. Those nearest the windows pressed close so they might report the purchases to those so unfortunate as to be in the rear. If they had not seen how much all of this meant to Katharine, shy Will and Orv would have fled to the shelter of their hotel. But Katharine beamed at the eager Parisians who surrounded her brothers.

Autograph albums appeared as by magic. Wilbur was appalled to have them thrust in his hands. He had not even seen one since he was in the eighth grade! He turned to Katharine. "What am I supposed to do with these things? I can't write 'Roses are red, Violets are blue' in all of them."

Katharine laughed gaily. "Of course not. Anyway, you don't know these girls. Just write your name; that's enough." She looked about at the city whose very skyline held such enchantment for her. "You might write, 'Wilbur Wright, Paris, 1909.'"

Safely back in the hotel, Katharine looked at the plain blue serge suit she was wearing. She opened the large oak wardrobe that filled one bedroom wall. The few simple dresses she had hung there seemed lost in its cavernous depths. Katharine had not really thought much about clothes for the trip. She had been so busy nursing Orville after his accident and making sure that he would be able to come.

But she thought about them now. Everywhere she went with her brothers, people would stare at her. And what better place could there be to think of clothes? Paris! She would go shopping this afternoon, alone.

The next two weeks whirled by so quickly that it was not until she was settled in her train compartment next to her brothers that Katharine was able to sort out the days, like pieces of a puzzle. As the train rolled and swayed, speeding toward the Pyrenees, she was able at last to arrange her thoughts in orderly fashion.

"What did you like best?" her brothers had asked, as Paris was left behind and the soaring spans of the Eiffel Tower disappeared from view.

"I liked everything best," she answered truthfully. For everything had been best in its way—morning service in Notre Dame, pictures in the Louvre, dinner at Maxim's, and the Opera. How could she choose?

"Did you hear what I said, Katharine?" Orville was reading a Paris paper. Wilbur never bothered with French, but Orville could read it well enough to make out most of the news.

Katharine jumped; her thoughts had been so far away.

"Just listen to this!" exclaimed Orville. Katharine had not heard that bubbling tone in Orville's voice since his accident. "The Court Circular announces that King Alfonso of Spain will spend some time in Pau to see flights in the Wright aeroplane. King Edward VII of England will also visit Pau this winter with members of his court. What do you think of that?" Orville shouted above the noise of the train.

"I think it is wonderful, just wonderful," his sister replied happily. And speaking to herself, she added, "How timely that I bought those dresses!"

A plain just outside the ancient city of Pau was selected as a flying field where Wilbur was to train three young French pilots. This quaint old town was a favorite resort in winter, for it was sheltered from storms by the circle of the Pyrenees Mountains near the border of Spain. Protected from winter winds, the open plain seemed an ideal place for the world's first flying lessons.

Katharine and Orville stayed at a hotel in the center of town, but Wilbur insisted upon living in the hangar, just as he had done at Le Mans. When the

mayor of Pau heard about Will's plan, he was dis-
tracted. This was no way for a famous man to live—a
man whose presence in Pau was so great an honor!
But Wilbur could not be persuaded to move.

If he refuses to be well-housed, at least he shall
be well-fed, the little mayor determined. He sent to
the hangar his own chef, who cooked fabulous dishes
for Wilbur and any guests who were at the field at
mealtime.

Katharine could not be glad enough that she had
added to her wardrobe. For as soon as it became
known that the Wrights were actually flying at Pau,
celebrities began to arrive from all over Europe.

The king of Spain lived nearest, so he was the
first to come. He reserved a suite of rooms in the hotel where Katharine and Orville were living. When
Katharine heard that he was really coming, she began
practicing a curtsy before the long mirror in her room.

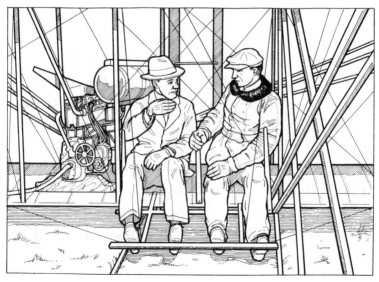

But there was no need. The king shook her hand and invited her and her brothers to luncheon.

King Alfonso very much wanted to ride in the plane, but his Cabinet had made him promise that he would not take such a risk. So he sat in the plane for more than an hour as it rested on the ground, asking dozens of questions about flying.

The Wrights had just said good-bye to one king when they had to be ready to greet another. King Edward of England came in March to see the fliers and their machine. This time, Katharine really practiced, for she was sure that she would be expected to make a curtsy. But once more her hand was vigorously shaken, instead.

Wilbur made a flight before King Edward, and when he landed he said, "Katharine, wouldn't you like a ride?"

Katharine was wearing her best new Paris hat in honor of the king's visit. It was a large hat, covered with long, curling ostrich plumes. She had worn her best dress, too, far from a flying costume.

"Oh, Will, I couldn't! My hat! And my dress is so long!"

But her brothers had planned this surprise. They meant to honor her in the presence of the king. Orville came forward pulling a veil from his pocket and a cord to tie down her full skirts.

Before the king and the members of his court, Katharine stepped into the open plane and sat beside Wilbur. Orville waved happily while the plane rose.

As she flew through the violet shadows of the late afternoon, Katharine's thoughts went back once more to the house on Hawthorne Street. She remembered all of the things her brothers had made there—the kites, the lathe, their first printing press. How proud their mother was then! How proud she would be now!

She remembered the green lawn covered with muslin as Will sewed on her machine the wings for his first flight. She remembered the warmed-over meals, as Will and Orv worked on the wind tunnel.

She remembered Father Wright's dollar. She remembered the neighbors—their scorn because her brothers would not give up their foolish notion that some day men would fly.

Now the years of struggle and worry, the years of sacrifice and uncertainty seemed to drop away as she felt the pulsing creature of their dreams—her dream as well as Will's and Orv's—fly toward the snow-capped mountains.

Katharine thought of the honors that were planned for her brothers—honors in Rome and in London, in New York and in Washington—and in Dayton, two days of celebration when they would ride through the familiar streets in a carriage drawn by white horses.

But no honors could bring more joy than the three together shared this day. At last, the ancient prophecy was fulfilled, "They shall mount upon wings as eagles...."

CHRONOLOGY

1867 — Wilbur Wright is born April 16 in Millville, Indiana.

1870 — Family moves to Dayton, Ohio.

1871 — Orville Wright is born August 19 in Dayton.

1878 — Family moves to Cedar Rapids, Iowa. Milton Wright brings his sons a toy helicopter.

1884 — Wrights move back to Dayton.

1886 — Wilbur is injured in a skating accident, interfering with his plans for college.

1889 — The boys start a printing business. Their mother, Susan, dies July 4. Orville decides to quit school.

1892 — The brothers open a bicycle shop called the Wright Cycle Co.

1896 — Orville seriously ill with typhoid fever for six weeks. Wilbur reads about the death of a famous glider pilot and becomes interested in flying. The brothers begin to manufacture their own brand of bicycles.

1899 — On May 30, Wilbur writes to Smithsonian Institution for information about aeronautics. The brothers construct and test a biplane kite.

1900 — The brothers test their first glider at Kitty Hawk, North Carolina, in September and October.

1901 — They return to Kitty Hawk to test a new, larger glider in July and August. They build a wind tunnel to test the drag and lift of various wing shapes.

1902 — They return to Kitty Hawk with their third glider in September and October. They set a number of world records.

1903 — The brothers return to Kitty Hawk. On December 17, Orville makes the first flight in a powered machine.

1904 — They move their testing to Huffman Prairie, a pasture east of Dayton.

1905 — They perfect their airplane and begin looking for buyers for their invention.

1906 — U.S. patent granted.

1908 — On February 10, 1908, the brothers win army bid to demonstrate flying machine and train pilots. They return to Kitty Hawk to test their newest Flyer in April. On May 14, they take up their first passenger. By the end of the month, Wilbur goes to France to demonstrate the airplane and breaks many records. On September 17, Orville demonstrates the Wright Flyer for the U.S. Army at Fort Myer, Virginia; but the plane crashes, killing Lt. Selfridge and severely injuring Orville.

1909 — Orville and his sister join Wilbur in Europe. The brothers are welcomed home to Dayton in a two-day celebration in which they are given a congressional gold medal. The Wright Co. is formed.

1910 — Orville begins flying schools near Montgomery, Alabama, and Dayton.

1911 — The U.S. government approves military aviation for the first time and establishes the first military flying school at College Park, Maryland. The brothers return to Kitty Hawk to test a new glider.

1912 — On May 30, Wilbur dies of typhoid at 45.

1915 — Orville buys the Wright Co. outright.

1916 — The airplane makes its mark in World War I. A controversy begins between Orville and the Smithsonian Institution, which billed Samuel P. Langley's Aerodrome as "the first man-carrying aeroplane in the history of the world capable of sustained free flight."

1917 — On April 3, Milton Wright dies at age 88.

1918 — Orville makes his last flight as a pilot.

1923 — Orville agrees to send the original 1903 Flyer to a London museum.

1928 — The original Flyer is shipped to London.

1932 — On March 3, a national monument to the Wright Brothers is dedicated at Kitty Hawk.

1948 — On January 30, Orville dies at age 77. On December 17, the Flyer is returned to the U.S. and is placed in the Smithsonian Institution.

Sources: Henry Ford Museum and Greenfield Village and News & Record research.